QUEER JIHAD

LGBT Muslims on Coming Out, Activism, and the Faith

ORACLE RELEASING

AFDHERE JAMA
AUTHOR OF "ILLEGAL CITIZENS: QUEER LIVES IN THE MUSLIM WORLD"

AN ORACLE RELEASING BOOK

Published in the United States of America by Oracle Releasing, LLC. Reach us on the web at www.OracleReleasing.com

No part of this publication can be reproduced, stored, or transmitted in any form or means, without permission from the publisher. The publisher assumes no responsibility for errors or omissions, or for damages resulting from the use of information contained herein.

Copyright © 2013 by the author. All rights reserved.

Cover design by Kemal Sharif.

Queer Jihad

QUEER JIHAD

By Afdhere Jama

Table of Content

Dedication 9

Acknowledging the Struggle 11

SULAYMAN X 15

DAAYIEE ABDULLAH 23

MUHSIN HENDRICKS 33

SURINA KHAN 41

OMAR NAHAS 49

EL-FAROUK KHAKI 55

FAISAL ALAM 73

ARSHAM PARSI 83

SCOTT "SIRAJ" KUGLE 91

LUDOVIC-MOHAMED ZAHED 103

HADIYO JIM'ALE 111

RUSLAN SHARIPOV 117

IAN IQBAL RASHID 125

ROB "SALIM" NASH 131

YASMENE JABAR 139

BADRUDDIN KHAN 147

WAEL K. 151

FARZANA DOCTOR 161

RAHAL EKS 169

FARIS MALIK 179

SHARIFA ISMAIL 185

About the Author 191

Glossary of Terms 193

Suggested Readings 195

Dedication

For the Friends on the Path of Struggle

Acknowledging the Struggle

There are so many people who contributed to the text that has become this book. Some have contributed their language by answering my questions, others have helped edit it, and there are those who facilitated some of these interviews, who introduced me to some of these people. This project came about through many channels, and I'm grateful for all of those who contributed in the so many different ways that they have.

For me, personally, it all started with Sulayman X and his website "Queer Jihad," which totally changed my life in the sense that I then was able to understand there were others like me out "there." When I say others like me I'm not talking about the way many people say, "Oh, I didn't know there were other queer Muslims in the world," no, I mean in the sense that I understood there were other queer Muslims who were not giving up on their lives, their sexuality, or their faith simply because some dude at their mosque said so. I'm talking about the fact that I realized there was a *jihad* going on, a real struggle.

So, it was no surprise to me that the title of this book had become the same as that of Sulayman's project, because the projects are different—his was about personal way of understanding, mine was more about through others—but the spirit is the same, the *jihad*, the struggle.

Therefore, a big thanks to Sulayman X.

Even though the idea to interview queer Muslims who are on the path of struggle came to me when I first read Sulayman's website, the real work really began with *Huriyah*, the queer Muslim magazine I founded and was the main editor at. Through the magazine I was able to interview these individuals, and actually put their interviews to use by sharing it with queer Muslim readers on a regular basis. With the exception of few, these interviews were conducted for and published in *Huriyah* between 2000 and 2010, where they constituted the main feature in each issue.

Queer Jihad

And, of course, *Huriyah* was not all me. Therefore, I wish to thank Abu Omar, my Arabic editor, whose dedication has made the magazine a success. I wish to thank Sharifa Ismail, our main financial supporter for the Arabic edition, whose support allowed us to continue year after year. I wish to thank J. S. Omar, my managing editor, who really managed gracefully and with love. I wish to thank all of the individuals who supported the magazine, the columnists, the writers, the information gatherers, the distribution managers, the readers and friends who advised us what we needed to change and what we needed to keep, all of those who helped us to continue for so many years.

The people in this book, these interview "subjects," they truly are the core of a community that has proved itself to be a revolutionary on course. The queer Muslim community, for the first time since the message of Islam has come to humanity in the 7th Century, has stood up in the lifetime of these people and has said, "No, Sir, we will not accept your interpretation of our faith, or allow you to define for us our lives," all through the collective *struggle* of their lives.

I want to thank you all, all of you, for standing up for your lives, for inspiring a new generation of our community to do the same, and for allowing yourselves to be part of a historic time in our faith.

"What is so important about these people?" asked a friend of mine, after I told him the book was being put together.

You tell me: some of these people are the first openly gay spiritual leaders, some are pioneers in organizations that were the first ones to offer support to queer Muslims, some of these people have written works that for the first time address queer sexuality and Islam in a serious and academic way, some of these people have been arrested and tortured in their countries and they still refused to deny their sexuality, some of these people have risked their very lives by negotiating with governments that had previously executed gays, and some of these people have created works of art that inspire us and show us that we too matter enough to see our reflections in film, music, or books.

Yes, maybe these people are not important to others, but to me, and to many other queer Muslims, they are very important. Their lives inspire a new generation of queer Muslims to also go out there and make a change in the world, starting in their own homes, with their families and their friends. That is "what is so important about these people."

Thank you all.

SULAYMAN X

In late 1996, I started looking for other queer Muslims online. I could not find anyone. Then I tried to find information on queer sexuality and Islam, and all I could find were negative information by Muslim scholars, who were totally ignorant on the subject, and homophobic people posting on different websites. As you can imagine, I was very disappointed. Later, in 1997, I found a small website called "Queer Jihad," it was by a Muslim convert named Sulayman X. At the time, the queer Muslims I had met in real life were mostly self-hating people, who were on the trip of "I'm a sinner" blues, which was why I went online in the first place. But Queer Jihad proved to be otherwise. This was a website by someone who was honestly on the road to accepting himself. Even though the author sounded like he was a lot older than I was, I felt I was connected to him. The website has turned into a wonderful haven for many others over the years. Thousands of people have e-mailed him about it, although much of it negative. So, when I set out to interview Sulayman X I was not just out to interview another gay Muslim but a man who had become a role model for many, and whose website's title would become the very title of this project.

When someone converts to Islam, some Muslims give him or her a "Muslim" name. I understand your name holds more than that for you.

When I converted to Islam in my 20s, I chose the name Sulayman (Solomon) because of its connotations with wisdom and knowledge. The brothers at the mosque who received my *shahada* insisted that I have two names, not just one, so they added Muhammad on to it, so my Muslim name became Sulayman Muhammad. That was all well and good, but then I began to learn that the Prophet Muhammad supposedly said things like, "If you come across two men doing what Lot's people did, kill the one who's doing it and the one it's being done to," or "Homosexuals should be thrown off the tops of high buildings," or

Queer Jihad

"Homosexuals should be driven from your midst," and so on and so forth.

These comments began coming just as soon as I set up the Queer Jihad web site—day after day I received messages telling me that this or that *hadith* said, "Muhammad said homosexuals should be killed wherever you find them" and all the rest of it, and I got to the point where I was sickened by the thought that the Prophet had actually said such things, so I dropped that name and replaced it with "X." Of course, the Nation of Islam people do that. They drop their last name, usually given to them by a former slave owner, and replace it with "X" as a sign of protest, as a way of saying they will no longer let themselves be defined by others. I did it for the same reason—why would I want to be known by the name of someone so outrageously homophobic?

Then I stumbled across the whole hadith mess, learning that there were some Muslims who questioned hadith, questioned some of the more outrageous sayings attributed to the Prophet, with some thinkers and groups rejecting hadith altogether. As a convert, one is not always clued in on all the various aspects of a particular religion, and there were a lot of stuff about Islam I didn't know (and still don't know!). This hadith controversy was one of them. My gut feeling, even before learning about the hadith problem, was that a man of Muhammad's spiritual stature simply would not have gone around saying such things about gay people, or any other group of people. A spiritually inclined and aware man or woman just doesn't go around advocating the killing of certain types of people. In the Prophet's case, the evidence as to his character, his judgment, his life, all said quite the contrary, and that to attribute such statements to him is way out of line.

As you noted, most converts don't realize the reality of the community might be different from what they had been told or exposed to. The mainstream Muslim community is pretty homophobic. What are you thoughts on this?

When I converted to Islam, in the early 1990s, there wasn't that much literature available to me on the subject. It was hard to find even a copy of the Qur'an at a bookstore, much less anything in depth about the religion itself. This was also before the popularity of the Internet came along. Still, I did my best, and I read everything available to me, and nowhere was homosexuality mentioned. Not once. Even today, if you look at Islamic books, if you check the index in the back of the book, it's rarely mentioned. There's almost a complete silence on the matter.

I assumed, from the many introduction to Islam type books that I read, that Islam was not particularly concerned about the matter. Islam was described to me as peaceful, tolerant, rational, "no compulsion in religion" [a verse from the Qur'an], full of respect for human rights and dignity, reasonable, open and frank about sexual matters, concerned for the well being of everyone in society—it never occurred to me that Islam would be so fiercely and unbendingly homophobic. This is another issue, all by itself.

These books, and the way they represent Islam, are simply not true to reality. They present the ideal, but not the truth of how things actually are, and because of that, they are deceitful and dishonest. They present only the best side of Islam, only the best ideals, only the loftiest sentiments, but the convert finds, once they start rubbing shoulders with "Muslims," that these lofty sentiments are not the ones most Muslims live by. And it's what these books don't say, what they don't tell you, that really hurts.

It's one thing to talk about there being "no compulsion in religion," but to live it? That's not a reality for most Muslims, because Islam is often nothing but compulsion. Homosexuality was never discussed, never mentioned, and frankly I was too embarrassed to ask about it at the mosque I was attending. I assumed—wrongly—that any religion that was so peaceful and tolerant and rational and reasonable would surely know that gay people don't get to choose their sexuality, that they have every right to exist and be, that there is more to a person than their sexuality.

But I was wrong.

Honestly, what was I supposed to think? Here was a religion that was so pragmatic that it would allow a man to have multiple wives, if the situation warranted it. Who knew it was so terrified of

Queer Jihad

gay people that it would put words in the mouth of the Prophet to the effect that they should all be thrown off cliffs? But even in saying all this, I have to point out that the Islamic ideal does indeed have a place for gay people, even if the reality doesn't. In other words, there isn't anything within the official Islamic basics that says being gay is wrong or not permissible. It's all a matter of interpretation, and of understanding that what we mean by "homosexual" today is vastly different than what people in the past meant. Allah made us all the way we are, just as we should be. Why can't I be what Allah made me to be?

This is the *jihad* of every queer Muslim who comes to a different understanding than what has been presented. That brings me to the name of your project, "Queer Jihad" is the name you gave to your website and to the forum. I personally met people who had problem with the title. What does the title mean to you?

The name of the website can easily be misconstrued, of course, but it's not meant to be offensive. There are two general meanings for the word "jihad," and the most basic meaning is the "struggle with oneself"—to be good, to do good, to lead a decent life, to struggle with your lower nature. We all engage in this "jihad." Only in a secondary, highly technical sense, does "jihad" mean "holy war." Consequently, a "Queer Jihad" means the struggle that gay people go through to be who they are, to accept who they are, to understand who they are, to develop a response to it. Some don't like the word "queer," believing it to be derogatory, but it's the only word that includes not just gay men, but gay women, transsexuals, and all those who find themselves to be different from the mainstream.

I have read the responses in the archives of the Queer Jihad website, going back to 1997, and they are filled with so much hate. It's enough to drive any person to a path of self-hate. How did you deal with this?

At first, I didn't deal with this very well, I must confess. I was surprised, then outraged, then hurt, then disbelieving—all sorts of emotions. I could not understand how other Muslims could talk to another Muslim in that fashion. I could not understand the mentality, that they thought they were defending the honor of Islam by using vulgarity and curses and death threats. It was all very highly instructive, and points out many of the things that are wrong with Islam today—the most basic being that if you don't like something then kill it, curse it, attack it, and any means justifies the end.

After a couple years of this, though, I began to see and understand that these people were afraid of me. They were afraid of what I represent. They do not want to see the truth that I insist on telling. I understand that, and I learned to have compassion for that, to tone down my own rhetoric, to understand that some people are not able to cope with some things, some issues, some ideas, and that they are caught up in cultural ignorance or prejudice or whatever.

Some people cannot make the jump, cannot move on to a higher level. Some people can only deal in black and white, and all the gray shades frighten them. That's a choice they make. I choose something different. I choose to confront the contradiction, the taboo, the uncertainty, and the risk. I don't have a choice, actually, because I have to live with myself. And indeed, this hatred that is expressed toward me—the hatred that every gay person feels and experiences, no matter where they live; this rejection, this disapproval, the shame of being gay, the shame of being different—indeed, it has an effect. How could it not? How can you go through your whole life never being accepted, never being understood, being feared and hated and judged, the object of ridicule, the bearer of a shameful dirty secret you dare not tell—how can this not damage and hurt you?

I feel sorry for young gay people today, struggling to not only grow up and come to terms with life and all the other things that all kids go through, but to also, on top of all of that, to come to grips with their sexuality.

What would you like to see the gay Muslim community become?

Queer Jihad

I would like to see the gay Muslim community working together, educating each other, supporting each other, speaking up, and helping each other. And yet "gay Muslims" are often divided amongst themselves with a great deal of in-fighting and pettiness.

There is so much criticism from within the community directed at the community. Some say some of these are positive criticism. Do you believe criticism can be a positive thing at this stage in the gay Muslim community?

These criticisms—it doesn't matter about what—are understandable, because we are a community of people who are suffering, who are looked down upon, who are frustrated (sexually and otherwise), who are beaten up on by the majority. In time, when we grow stronger, we will be able to see things more clearly, and there will be room for tolerance and respect and wide range of viewpoints. But in the beginning, with such a group, it's always rough going. So many people are filled with doubts and spiritual torments. With such angst and anguish, what can you expect?

Do you identify with a particular path in Islam?

I do not think it's fair to define myself as a "Muslim," and I no longer do so. I have respect for all religions and for all people who make a sincere effort to love and serve God. I submit myself wholly and completely to Allah, to God. I believe Muhammad was the prophet of God, just as Jesus was, just as the Buddha was. There is only one "truth." There can only be one truth. Many different people have expressed it in different ways, but the fundamentals are the same. There are remarkable similarities in all the world's religions. Each of them asks that we submit ourselves to God and try to lead decent, good lives. Don't hurt other people. Take responsibility for your actions. Don't lie. Don't cheat. Don't steal things. Make God the center of your life. All these labels that we use are just dividing us—that's their point, isn't it? Muslim, Hindu, Christian, Buddhist. When we separate off into us and them, believing our group to be better than their group, then we have failed to understand what God is all about. Anyway, I'm happy to go to the mosque, but I also go to Mass sometimes, or the Hindu temple. Sometimes I just sit and meditate. God is everywhere, not just in some building, and certainly not the exclusive property of one group.

"I submit myself wholly and completely to Allah." Why, Sulayman, me thinks you are a Muslim. There are many types of Muslims, one doesn't have to define oneself by a label. You are a very spiritually inclined person. I always believed Sufism and Buddhism are from the same tree. What are some of the things that attract you to these paths?

Sufism and Buddhism—yes, I'm somewhere in between, not quite one, not quite the other. What attracts me to these paths? In Sufism, it's love. As a Sufi, you relate to Allah as your Beloved. When you start wandering down the path of love, you find the rules are different. Love doesn't permit cruelty. Love won't allow you to despise another person, no matter how bad that person is. Love won't allow you steal from another person, or hurt any living thing in any way. People who are in love are the happiest people. The world is full of color and life, and every little thing has meaning. Love is healing. Love keeps you humble and attentive to the one you love. Love teaches you to always seek what's best for others, to never harm, to let go of selfishness and smallness.

Buddhism, on the other hand, is about suffering. Buddhism itself is a series of teachings that have to do with suffering, and with how we can stop suffering. The Buddha was only human, and never claimed to be otherwise, and Buddhism has nothing to do with gods or demons or anything else. In that sense, Buddhism is not a "religion."

I've suffered a great deal in my life, and Buddhism helped me to make sense of it, and helped me to see how I could put a stop to all that suffering. I think most gay people suffer a great deal, and would find great solace and help in Buddhism, if they would open themselves to it and give it a chance. Suffering has to do with clinging and craving, with desires, with constant wanting and needing—all these things lead to suffering.

Queer Jihad

You have been celibate for many years and that has to do with the fact that you have a very Buddhist view to sexuality, desires, et cetera. Let's talk about that.

Eroticism and my response to that issue is very Buddhist, that the more you crave and desire, the more you will suffer. It doesn't matter what you crave or desire—drugs, porn, love, fame, wealth—you will suffer because of it. That's guaranteed. You can look at your own life for ample evidence. If you can learn to let go of craving, to be more accepting of reality as it is, you can learn how to stop suffering. You can learn to become content with how things are, rather than spending so much effort and energy trying to change everything.

Changing things, that brings me to my last question. In every interview that I do, I ask this last question: if you had the power to change something about yourself, what would it be and why?

I wouldn't change anything. We are who we are. Rather than wondering about what we could change, we should work on accepting what we are and moving on.

<u>UPDATE:</u> This interview was conducted in early 2002, and was published in November 2002 (on both the English and the Arabic editions of *Huriyah*). Since then, Sulayman X has written several books. These include "Bilal's Bread," and "The Adventures of a Bird-Shit Foreigner," both dealing with gay and immigrant themes. His first book in the Father Ananda series, "Mindfulness and Murder," has been adapted into a feature film with the same title and released in 2011.

DAAYIEE ABDULLAH

When I met Daayiee many years ago, I realized he was one of those rare individuals that you feel you're lucky to meet. He's just a very unique person. Born and raised in Michigan, within a Baptist environment, Daayiee Abdullah traveled literally to the other side of the world in China to find Islam. Today, he lives to study Islam and educate Muslims and non-Muslims about his faith, sexuality, and gender related issues. Strong in his conviction, he's just one of those people you can't help but admire. He is a good spiritual leader, who does not shy away from giving you a good advice.

The name "Daayiee," what does it mean and how did it come to you?

First, "Daayiee" means to call—to call to the religion. It rhymes with my Chinese name "Daee," which means a man of great virtue. And since I was introduced to Islam in China, I felt that my Chinese name going to a Muslim name had to collocate a particular meaning in a particular sense of spirit.

Where were you born, and where did you grow up?

I was born in Detroit, Michigan, and grew up in Detroit. I did a lot of traveling in the United States and parts of Canada as a child, however.

I know you reverted to Islam later in your life, talk about your spiritual background prior to that.

I was raised in a Southern Baptist home. Both of my parents were Baptist. However, my parents were very liberal in their understanding of what religion meant. They didn't believe that their particular religion was the only way in which people can show their faith in God.

Was that unique in America at that time?

Queer Jihad

Yes, it was, but I think my parents were more highly educated than most. Though they were African-American, they both had their college education.

What did they study?

My mother went to college to teach and my father went in business.

This is a time when Black America was not accepted as much as today.

That is true. Well, my mother coming from a business family herself, she grew up with income. She was able to put herself through school. Mother was a distributor of black beauty products in Detroit. The city having a high population of African-Americans, my mother did hair in the funeral homes on the weekends during the depression. My father worked where he eventually received his business degree. So I had that type of determination about who we are as people.

Was there a reconciliation for you between being gay and Baptist Christian?

No. Actually when I was listening to—what I refer to as babblum—the many dogmatic interpretations given, even at young age, I felt that information was not accurate. Since I was very well educated early in life, even if I didn't understand them all, I knew how to ask intelligent questions. And many times when I would ask these questions, the adults whom I would ask, who were the "leaders" in the community and/or individuals such as my Pastor of the church, a lot of times those people couldn't answer my questions.

It's the dogma thing. Many religious folks all over the world don't have the answers to young people's contemporary questions.

That is correct. Very few people who I ran into in these institutions were able to intelligently answer my questions. I did have one gentleman, who was my scout leader, at my church, and he was open-minded, very well educated man. He took time to explain things to me and at least gave me the time to understand how the big picture worked.

Looking back, which was harder in mainstream America... being Gay or Black?

I think being Black, for myself, was most difficult part because I was an affirmative action child in the late 1960s and early 1970s when these opportunities became available as I had the requisite skills to enter into the corporate arena. However, there was the issue of lack of exposure generally on the part of the Whites rather than on my part. And, so, was on trial and error situations on many instances.

What has been your experience with the Black Muslims in America as a Gay Black man?

Well, it depends which strand of "Black Muslims" you are referring to. If you are talking about the Nation of Islam, frequently I find most of them are not very well educated either in the religion and/or the generally socially-accepted skills.

It's very interesting that you say that because when I came to this country, as a young African Muslim immigrant, I was extremely attracted to the Nation as people because they were generally well-dressed and their manners in public made me think they were well-educated as well. Is there something deeper you are referring to?

Well, I agree they have have a wonderful way of using Islam for good purposes. For example, when folks are converted in prison they tend to not go back. And they do dress well. So, they definitely have good graces. However, in terms of understanding the faith fully, many of them have—what I call—mulish mentality, where they read a book or two and they think they know everything about Islam. That is their downfall because of lack of education. Not all of them are that way but a large number of them that I ran into are.

Then there are those African-American Muslims who were once part of the Nation of Islam and went over to NAMA (North

American Muslim Association). I think there is a different association with them as they tend to be more traditionally trained. Even though some of them are *salafi* trained or oriented teaching, I find that some of them can utilize that "training" and apply it to their lives as African-Americans in America.

Including gay African-Americans?

I think for some, yes. Overall, as I meet more and more traditionally trained and we talk. At least we have some close references because we both have that background.

As a Black Muslim of Christian background, what were your first experiences with immigrant and/or children of immigrant Muslims in America?

I had many experience with immigrant Muslims before I became Muslim. That exposure happened to me in college for the most in terms of meeting people who were either first generation or children of first generation in America. Some of these people were those who immigrated to America eight or nine years earlier, so they had their old home traditions. And from there I found there was a greater sincerity in which a number of them approached their religion. I found that to be a pillar for me to look at what Islam meant. And some of those exposures definitely helped me solidify my sense of faith in Islam.

I know you traveled around the Muslim world, did you find differences between immigrant Muslims in America and those back home?

Yes, many differences. I think that overall there is a difference in education exposure and exposure to other people. Generally unless they are part of a certain economic or social level, the Muslims in those countries don't have exposure or access to others. I'm not talking about those who live in big cities like Cairo and the such. When they ran across me as someone who converted to Islam, it is not my blackness that they find unusual but that I'm an American. And then when they found out I did so in China, that even blows their minds. So we always have a joke that goes "Allah will find you wherever you are, even in China."

You started out in the legal profession, why did you choose law?

Law is a very important aspect of things. Of my particular educations, I think Law was the one that helped me the most expand my imagination to its fullest because I had to start learning and thinking on different level. Prior to studying Law, I was somewhat core-oriented but I was limited to the pages (of Scriptures) but I think Law pumped up my thinking.

You studied Islam and became a *sheikh*, or scholar, why did you choose to study Islam so extensively?

I think for my own personal edification. I needed to know exactly how the term "Homosexuality" is viewed in *Sharia* and also by the Holy Qur'an. You see, the Holy Qur'an gives us message and then the Sharia is the human interpretation of it. I wanted to be more aware of all these things in a more detailed setting.

Did your non-Islamic Law background help you?

Yes, it did. It helped me look at the same kinds of themes. The Law here is Judeo-Christian and, as you know, that is Abrahamic. Their foundations come from the same bases. So I was able to cross-reference amongst the three religions.

Briefly, could you tell me your view of Islam's attitude towards sexuality in general?

As I understand it, the Qur'an states that sexuality is one of the benefits that God gives to us as human beings. Many people take that to mean the aspect of procreations. However, I think it is broader than that. There is also enjoyment. Some people may not be able to procreate but they have the enjoyment of sexuality. This enjoyment is best in the form of commitment or marriage.

In the west, we have heard many times folks accusing Islam of being a sexophobic of sort. What do you say to people like that?

I think they are wrong about that. I think in Islam sexuality is different than that of the Christian west. In the west, sexuality is open. In Muslim cultures, it is more private. So when they say Islam is sexophobic they are actually judging by their own standard. Both of them have their benefits and problems. In the vast majority of the Muslim countries, there is low rate of rape and self-esteem. On the other hand, in the west it is more open for people who want to do things together. I like to think, personally, that it is better to live in part of the world where a woman is not afraid of me walking on the same street as her just because I'm a man. And, unfortunately, that is the case in the west. Over there, men respect women far more because society demands it.

And, in your view, what is Islam's attitude towards homosexuality?

Basically, what people have been trained to believe has been that homosexuality is incompatible with Islam. The basis that they use is that it is not natural, it goes against social order and that it brings disease. All three are incorrect. First, the natural order thing, that particular one is based on procreation. And, like I said earlier, that has holes in it. Although many heterosexual couples can bear children, not all can have children. Second, they say it goes against social order. Well, that particular part is correct for heterosexuals. And the problem with that is they assume social order in heterosexual normative because that is how the Qur'an speaks as the majority is heterosexual. And the third point that they make is absolutely bogus. Disease befalls all those it befalls regardless of sexual preference.

Why is the majority of the Muslim World so publicly homophobic?

It is what they are trained to do. It is like some of the African-Americans in this country; they always think that white people are doing something to them, or that white people are naturally bad or something like that, which has no basis in scientific fact or anything of that nature. So the Muslims have been trained that way. You will see in some cultures children being separated at the age of seven because people fear they will turn into this thing. It is like the bogeyman. And later some of the homosexual young men start thinking they are this bogeyman and society shames them, beats them and sometimes kills them. And sometimes these young men commit suicide themselves because they can't accept the pressure. It is horrible.

Where do you think this irrational fear of homosexuality comes from in some of these modern Muslim countries?

I think large part of it is face. Ancient societies have this face to protect in public. What anyone says or does in the back of their bedroom is different issue. When I lived in Cairo, I lived in this building and one of my classmates told me there was prostitution going on. I said, "Well, how do you know?" And he told me that he was approached several times. But these women all wore *hijab* during the day. It is face.

Do you think there will be time when the majority of the Muslim World becomes accepting of queer sexuality?

Of course! As they are exposed to it more in different atmosphere. It will take sometime. One thing I saw when I was teaching in Saudi Arabia is that there are a number of Muslims who find it easier to not think about certain things. They want to follow what others say.

I know you are doing a lot of work in America to help change the gap between queer and straight Muslims. How is that going?

It is going fairly well. I believe Allah's concept for us is not exclusive, which has been the venue that many people utilized. "We are here and they are there, therefore they are not like us and we are better than they are." I think that is very limited. What I have learned is that a better way to get people to understand each other is to show where our similarities are. I try to get people to understand that we are going to have differences whether it is the color of our skin or the gender of our bodies, the sexual orientation of our minds, the educational levels and everything else that makes us diverse. Allah on this planet is six billion different expressions.

You have been doing marriage officiating, both for straight and queer Muslims, what has been the straight

Queer Jihad

Muslims' attitude towards a gay imam performing something they hold so sacred?

I believe they feel, because of my particular position, that I would understand why they feel their spiritual person in the Mosque are limiting what they do and who they do it for. And these men and women are willing to withdraw from those kinds of services. They don't want that anymore. They are tired of it. They want their services to be done by broader-thinking people like myself.

What is your relationship with the "straight" mosques?

If I go to the Mosque I generally tend to not linger a whole lot. In Washington, a number of people know who I am. I don't give them the opportunity to gang on me, if you will, but I also don't let them intimidate me either. They don't own the Mosque though they may own the space.

I know you are planning to open an inclusive mosque. What has been the queer Muslim community's response to that?

I will have to say that in other cities, such as Toronto, it has been a good response. I was over there last November helping them get start on their program. Philadelphia just started recently and I believe folks in San Francisco are doing the same. In Washington, I find it that people shy away from it. I'm hoping that I will reconnect with people and see if they are willing to get involved again. I'm also trying to find a building, or people who would donate a space like that.

Do you think this type of mosque will be successful?

Yes because our concept is extensive and broad. People of different sexualities and genders can participate in the rituals, which I believe will draw people.

Now totally different subject, talk about casual sex.

Well, as far as I'm concerned, I don't think that kind of sex has been good, though it has happened to me. I don't think it is the best formulation because I believe you are letting your lust get the best of you.

In your opinion, is it more important to have love or compatibility in a relationship?

I think it is important that you have both of them. But which one should come first? I think compatibility builds and develops a greater love. It opens up ways for the couple to achieve success in the relationship.

I wanted to talk to you about same-sex marriages. I know you and brother Siraj Kugle were working on the marriage question for queer Muslims and came to a rather interesting position.

We have come to a certain position on it. The work is not completely done yet as I'm still working on my portion of it. We are looking from different points of view such as a social justice part as well as legal side. The main thing is that the way Islam views relationships is very different from the way other religions view relationships. Relationships in Islam are more inclusive. So marriage is a good thing no matter who you are.

In every interview that I do, I ask this last question: if you had the power to change something about yourself, what would it be and why?

Wow. That is an interesting question. I have different areas that I would like to work on since I'm not perfect.

UPDATE: Since this interview was conducted in 2002, Daayiee Abdullah joined forces with the Muslims for Progressive Values (MPV), where he directs the LGBT Outreach Program, as well as being the imam of the inclusive mosque in the Washington, DC area, which is part of the inclusive mosques around the world that welcome LGBT Muslims openly in their congregation, membership, and leadership. His book "Queer Sexuality in Islam" is being published in early 2014 by Oracle Releasing. To learn more

Queer Jihad

about the book visit OracleReleasing.com, and to learn more about MPV visit mpvusa.org

MUHSIN HENDRICKS

I remember I was in a Muslim chat room when I was invited to read an article on a gay Muslim imam in South Africa. The article discussed how this man—an imam—defends queer Muslims. I couldn't believe my eyes! It was the first time I ever read about a Muslim religious leader, queer or otherwise, defending queer Muslims. I have known gay or bisexual imams before, but they were closeted and did not want to bring "attention" to themselves by standing up for queers. I admired Muhsin. He was clearly different, and when I interviewed him I realized he was someone who was going to change the world.

You have said before that your mother is your greatest supporter. Was she always supportive of your sexuality?

No, when I told her initially, she wanted to disown me. She said I was busy with Satan and she as a religious figure in our Community cannot have such a "thing" as a gay son on her doorsteps. We had lots of arguments, but now that she understands my pain and struggle, she's accepted it. She also accepted my relationship with a man who now calls her Mommy. However, she prefers us not to flaunt our sexuality and we respect that.

People assume acceptance means being part of everything. I think acceptance is just the person accepting you, without necessarily agreeing with you. How do you define acceptance?

There cannot be acceptance without tolerance. This is something we can learn from the character of our beloved prophet Muhammad, peace be upon him. He was even tolerant towards the disbelievers until Allah commanded him to be harsh against them for what they stand for. Unfortunately we do not have that kind of insight as to know what the intentions of others, who are different from us, are.

Accepting others does not mean that you have to invite them for dinner, but rather to respect their opinions and lifestyles. We should not set out to harm or belittle them, especially if they do not pose a threat to your own beliefs and space. Instead, we need to constantly seek Allah's guidance so that at least we ourselves are on the straight. Excuse the pun!

I heard your grandfather was an imam. Did you want to follow his footsteps?

I never wanted to follow his footsteps. He was too pedantic for my liking and I never liked him for the fact that he was preaching Orthodoxy, which I came to despise later. I always wanted to become an imam, as I thought that by educating myself I would be able to understand my making and my place in Islam as a gay Muslim.

You went to Pakistan to study Arabic and Islam. Why Pakistan?

I won a scholarship to study there. A blessing I must say! It was an Islamic scholarship from a South African ex-organization called "Call of Islam".

After you came out, you were stripped of your "sheikh" title. I don't think people have a right to do that, you have worked very hard for the title. Anyway, does it make any difference to you whether or not they stripped it off?

Other than the fact that it is painful to think that your community disregards you because of your sexuality, I still help and educate many who come to my doorstep. That is what I was destined to do. *Alhamdulillah*, I am contented with my lot.

Are all of your students queer?

No! Despite the fact that others know about my sexuality, they still come to me for spiritual advice.

You created an organization called "Al-Fitrah," which helps people spiritually. How did Al-Fitrah come to be and what do you guys do exactly? And, by the way, when was it created?

Al-Fitrah was created in October 1998 by five concerned members. Because of most guys being "in the closet" we did not have many committed helpers, which resulted in myself having to do all the work. I was burnt out and could not run the organization all by myself. In October 2001 a few guys asked me to restart the support groups, which I gladly did with some experience behind me.

Al-Fitrah took a new face, a more spiritual one, and this time it worked. We met every alternate Sunday where we had talks on spirituality and sexuality. We meditated and prayed together. We had *Muharram* programs as well as Ramadan programs.

Unfortunately for Al-Fitrah, because of my relationship, I had to move to Johannesburg where I am now concentrating on my book and developing the organization as an online organization for many reasons.

What are you beliefs about being queer?

In my understanding, a homosexual is a make-up of biology and environmental factors. The same applies to a heterosexual. So, irrespective whether our environment influences our psychological behavior, mankind's make-up is largely biological and *taqdir* (fate). Thus *Al-Fitrah* (the natural way of the Divine) aims to make the individual realize that he is innately a sexual being but at the same time he needs to take responsibility for his/her actions and to keep the relationship with the Creator constant. The individual's sexuality is but a fraction of who s/he is. It should not become the overriding factor in the individual's life. We were created to worship Allah, and we should do so with whatever fate we were handed.

I had a friend who lived in South Africa and he said a lot of good things about Al-Fitrah. In fact, I have met many people who know or know of Al-Fitrah and they never criticize you guys. Is there a kind of joy that comes with being accepted like that?

Good begets good! We at Al-Fitrah have Allah-consciousness as our main priority and we always start our activities in His name.

Queer Jihad

We are not a dating service, nor a club for lonely hearts. Al-Fitrah concerns itself largely with the development of the soul, as it has no gender. We have no other agendas and I think it is because of this that we are respected. We have helped many to find inner peace and in that we find fulfillment.

You once mentioned you had a case where a lesbian Muslim committed suicide because she couldn't handle dealing with the "two" identities. Please, tell us more about that.

She came from a very Orthodox family. They would not accept her and did not even visit her at her flat. Although she had relationships with other women, she was lonely and felt rejected. The pain was too much for her. She was found dead, by a family member, on her prayer mat, after three days. She took an overdose of sleeping pills. Incidentally, this episode also made my mother realize that homosexuality cannot be a choice.

What would you like to see the queer Muslims community working towards in achieving?

Unfortunately contemporary gay culture leaves much to be desired in the eyes of the larger Muslim community. The flamboyancy, indecency, and licentiousness associated with us leave a bad taste with these Muslims, including myself. What I propose we—as Muslim Homosexuals, Bisexuals and Transgender—do is to create a culture that will be respected by our Muslim brethren. I have done it in my personal life and I have managed to change the thinking of certain Muslims about homosexuality. We can be respected if only we portray a more Allah-conscious and purer lifestyle.

I always feel like I'm queer first because I choose to be a Muslim. I'm open to be taught, so tell me about this. Which comes first, in your opinion?

Everything that exists is born in a state of *fitrah* (natural submission to Allah's will). We have two kinds of submission; voluntary and involuntary submission. The former is where we choose to worship Him and follow His commands, such as fasting, praying etc. In the latter, we have no choice. We have to breathe, eat, sleep, etc. Apple trees do not bear oranges. The sun does not shine at night, etc. So, in this respect we are involuntarily submitting to Allah's will (Muslim).

In order for us to become complete Muslim, we need to bring our "Freedom or Choice" in submission to His will as well. My sexuality is an involuntary aspect of my being. I have no choice in the matter. Accepting my sexuality as *fitrah* and not trying to fight it, means submitting to Allah's will. How I act out my sexuality is my choice. In my choice and actions, I am Muslim first, and then a being that needs to be sexually gratified.

You have discussed something on your website that I would like to have you talk about. What are the differences between homosexuality, sodomy, and sexual perversion?

I cannot be brief in this matter as these are not easy phenomena to explain. Let me put it this way: Homosexuality is an Allah-given sexuality. You have no choice in the matter. You might not act out your sexuality, but it does not make you "straight."

Sodomy according the Qur'anic rendition of the Sodom & Gomorrah story is male to male rape, involving power and humiliation. This is not *fitrah*, it is a choice.

Sexual perversion has very little to do with the sexuality of an individual, but the individual's state of mind. Sexual perversion is also a perception. What might be sexual perversion to some is normal to others. Some might see fellatio and anal sex as sexual perversions while to others it's pretty normal. Bestiality to some is sexual perversion, while in some it's the ritual of unity with the animal kingdom. In the matter of personal taste versus sexual perversion, the Muslim decides what it is that brings him closer to Allah and what it is that makes him become slave to his passion.

As you are aware, we have some hadiths that say unkind words about queer people. What are your beliefs on these hadiths?

Although Qur'an and Hadith are both trustworthy sources, Hadith does not have the dynamism and flexibility of the Qur'an.

Hadith are second hand narratives and subject to culture, time, background and mood; while the Qur'an can be interpreted into many cultures, different times and does not have a single mood. There are hadiths, seemingly condemning Homosexuality. Similarly, there are empathic hadiths regarding "eunuchs" and "males who have no desire for the opposite sex". This, largely depend upon the situation the Prophet was presented with.

If you weigh the two, you will notice a strong sense of sexuality versus sodomy, and the Prophet being compassionate towards the former and stern against the latter. Had there ever been a case of a man coming to the Prophet and stating his homosexuality, and the pain associated with it, we would have seen the compassion of the prophet in this regard and today we would have earned the respect of the Muslim community.

Retrospectively, the status quo is a blessing to those homosexuals who have magnified sexual needs. Just imagine! Also bear in mind that there were no persecutions of homosexuals in the time of the Prophet.

But the majority of the Muslims of today do not see that. I mean, while you and I, and many others, realize that there is no way the hadiths can have same standards as that of the Qur'an, traditional Muslims still argue that hadiths are extremely authentic. Do you think this will ever change?

Muslims don't take too easy to change. They are afraid of losing the essence of being Muslim, but what they do not realize is that by not allowing change, while still keeping the principals of Islam in tact, they are inadvertently destroying the dynamism of Islam in that it can be interpreted to accommodate the needs of any specific culture or time. Muslims practice Islam as an "Arabized" religion. Islam gave birth in an Arabian Culture, but it is not an Arabic religion. For this reason Muslims find it difficult to apply Islam to contemporary western culture.

Many gay Muslims, as odd as it may sound to some, accept themselves as gays but do not accept homosexual sex. What are your beliefs about homosexual sex?

How does one make sense of the fact that Allah does not lay on you a burden greater than what you can bear and at the same time he creates sexual gratification as a basic human need. Are we as homosexuals being punished even before the act is committed? Remember that it is the public display of sexual activity, with witnesses, that is punishable according to the Quran.

Whatever happens in privacy is a matter between the two individuals involved and their Creator. Remember that there was also the prostitute who was forgiven due to her compassion towards a thirsty animal. Remember there was also the innocent killing of men and women charged for sexual indecency during the Caliphate. There was also the granting of temporary marriage (max 3 days & 3 nights) for the sole purpose of sexual gratification during war. And so there were many exceptions made in the name of sex.

Allah-consciousness is what should always prevail in any decision. And as the Prophet said, "Amongst the first prophecies was: If you do not feel any shame, then do as you please!"

Let us not decide what's good for individuals and what's not. But let us encourage one another to more good for our souls because it is the soul that lives on and it is the actions of the body that determines the destination of the soul.

Are you in a romantic relationship?

Yes, Alhamdulillah! As all relationships have its ups and downs, this one has too. But as long as I'm growing, I'm happy.

What are you thoughts on same-sex marriage?

I prefer calling it a "same-sex commitment". The word "marriage" is too sacrosanct in many cultures, yet it should not be like that in Islam. Marriage in Islam is a contract just like any other business contract. You have the *wakeel* (lawyer), the *ijaab* (request), the *qabul* (the acceptance of the request), the *ahd* (contract), and the *shuhada* (witnesses). Whatever is added to this is superficial. We make marriage a holy affair. As regards to two people of the same sex having a "contract" to live together, grow together and share in the lives of one another and share the responsibilities attached to it, I have no problem with that, but to base such a commitment on the same pattern as a heterosexual marriage is preposterous. Although the contract might be similar, the dynamics are different.

Do you have any regrets?

Yes, I've wasted lots of time.

What do you mean you wasted a lot of time, you are still very young.

Because of my sexuality, I became withdrawn as a teenager. I spent a lot of time crying and resenting myself for who I am. I could have used that time constructively. I lost my teenage years because of that. There is a positive side to it though. If I did not have that experience, I would not have had the desire to save other teenagers from the agony of resenting themselves for who they are.

In every interview that I do, I ask this last question: if you had the power to change something about yourself, what would it be and why?

And as I answer this question in almost every interview; nothing! I believe that one needs to make do with whatever has been handed to you by fate.

UPDATE: Since this interview was conducted in 2003, Muhsin had closed down *Al-Fitrah* and created *The Inner Circle*, which has had many international conferences, has local spiritual presence, and even published a book. It's one of the few organizations that has had the success of being recognized on a global scale.

SURINA KHAN

Surina Khan is one of the few prominent women of color in the LGBT movement in the United States. For many years, she worked to advance LGBT and Women's Rights in various organizations. She was the Executive Director of the Gay and Lesbian Human Rights Commission, the vice president of the Women's Foundation of California, and garnered praise as a research analyst for the Political Research Associates. Her work has taken her around the world, but she's a down to earth woman who deeply values freedom, justice, and love.

What does your name mean?

I'm not sure what it means, actually, but I know that my mother read my name in the paper. There were two princesses that were born in Malaysia by the time I was being born. One was named Surina and one was named Suraya, and she happened to like the name Surina. The two were named after stars in the sky.

Where in Pakistan were you born?

I was born in Karachi.

I heard your family left Pakistan after your father was accused of being spy for the United States. Is that true?

I think that is what happened. We left the winter of 1972 and Bhutto was in power. And my uncle, my father's older bother, had a political party that was an opposition to Bhutto. So, even though my parents were not politically active particularly, their relationship to my uncle and my father's business ties to the US put him in danger, and so we left the country.

How hard was it moving here?

I think it was pretty hard for most of my family, not so much for me because I was really young, but I think to sort of pick up and having to leave suddenly without even packing a house, not knowing what was gonna happen and not being used to the cultural difference; certainly the way that translated into language, cooking, and the space. For me, I was young, so it wasn't that much of a big deal.

I once read an article in which you said you grew up thinking you were a rich white girl. How did that happen to a Pakistani girl who was not even born in America?

We were living in Connecticut, which was really white. For example, our street was all white except for our family. And I went to an all-girl boarding school, which did have some people of color but not many. So, I really, in an effort to assimilate and feel comfortable in my surrounding, which I think is a natural to a child and someone new who just wants to fit in, that sort of assimilation made me really relate to white people.

I think it's totally understandable.

Yes, it's understandable, but it's also unfortunate and experience many people probably go through. And it's something, I think, that if you look at the Right Wing politics in this country—when they try to do away with bilingual education or multiculturalism—what they really are trying to say is that if you can identify and act like a good white person then you're allowed to be a person of color. It was that sort of thing that I was buying into.

After living in the United States most of your life, you went back to Pakistan at the age of eleven. How did you feel being there after having being "Americanized"?

There are differences. On many levels, it was very comfortable for me because there were old family friends. It was easy to fall back into life there. It was familiar. I knew the people as I had so many family members there. But at the same time, I'm very much sort of a bicultural person. I have grown up here and there. There is a sort of trans-national aspect of my life that can go back and forth and feel very comfortable at those cultures.

When did you first start identifying yourself as a lesbian? I don't mean to others, I mean to yourself?

Well, I will tell you the first time that I thought about it. I was very young, I think I was about eight years old, and it just popped into my head and I wondered whether—I think I just felt the attraction towards other girls, and to women—so I wondered would I grow up being attracted to women. I thought that was a crazy thing to be thinking of at eight years old. I put it out of my head, but it was always there and I grew up in a family that didn't really talk much about sexuality let alone homosexuality. And, so, when it was spoken it was spoken of in a very negative way.

So, were you able to identify what being a lesbian was instead of just your feelings? I mean, did you know there was such thing as a lesbian?

Yes, I did. Sure, when I was growing up, even as a young teenager, and I think that has to do with the fact that we were living here and not what I would call in a traditional home. I mean, even though Urdu was spoken in the home—and there were many parts of the culture that were there—my parents were quite liberal in terms of breaking us up, the education we all got. It wasn't really that we were shielded from issues of sexuality as it occurred to us in the broader world that we were living in. So, I did know but I also knew that it was called perverse and disgusting, so it was something that I really repressed. I thought that something was wrong with me and that it wasn't something I was going to pursue. Of course, until I fell in love with another woman and that is when I began that process of coming out to myself. And at that point I was about eighteen.

How did your family react when you came out to them?

They had a very difficult time. It was very painful for them and for me because it wasn't something they could understand. They didn't have any indication early on that this is something I might be. So, it was very difficult for them. My mother and I, especially, went through a long process. We didn't speak for a couple of years. I have a brother who didn't speak to me for ten years.

So, it was difficult, at the same time, now, I don't know about fifteen years later, certainly we have gone through a process. I'm very close to my sisters, and I was close to my mother before she died in 1999. The thing I really said to my mother was because of the strength and the upbringing that she gave me that I was able to live honestly with myself with the courage of convictions and the values she taught me.

Many people who are out to their family still keep "discreet" love life. Is that the case with you? Is your family aware of your love life?

Yes, they are. When I came out it was a huge relief to me, which I don't think even I expected. I thought that, maybe, it would still continue to feel burdensome, but it was a huge relief. And, for me, it was really based on my values system of honesty and that carried through to all parts of my life, so I never had to think twice about the fact that I was going to share every aspect of my life with my family. It was important for me to talk openly about my relationship and inviting people home. And, basically, not lying unless there was some, or I felt there was some, danger issues. My family is very aware of my relationship and, in fact, I think it is quite remarkable that they don't even seem to be uncomfortable and like my partner very much.

That's really nice. You don't hear about a lot of Muslim families that are like that, so it gives queer Muslims hope that their own families might accept them as well.

And that is really my sisters, because my extended family is another story. And the thing is that all you have to do is type my name in a Google search and you pretty much get my life history. They know that I was the director of IGLHRC. And, even whether they found out that on the Internet or when I had gone home, one of the first questions you get is "Where are you working?" So, for years, it wasn't that I wasn't out to them but I wasn't because it never came up in the context of anything important. When I was working at IGLHRC and they would ask me, I would tell them that I'm the director of the International Gay and Lesbian Human Rights Commission. Suddenly, it was like "Whoa!"

And I was kind of amazed at the reaction that I got in terms of when I was in a room and "Gay and lesbian? Oh, my God!" So, my way of dealing with it had to do with the way I was feeling personally at that point. I was a little tired of doing all this education all the time and I was home visiting my family and that was the purpose of my visit.

We are constantly doing all this teaching and sometimes teaching the same thing several times to the same person and what not. It is hard! It really gets irritating and tiresome.

Yes, I agree. What I said to them was, "If it makes you uncomfortable then we don't have to talk about it." And, actually, as it turned out, that turned out to be a really good strategic choice of words. As soon as I said that—and I said that to several cousins at different times—suddenly their guard went down and they were like, "Oh, yea, actually I'd like to talk about it."

How do you identify politically?

Politically I'm a lesbian, feminist and leftist-progressive activist.

Let's talk about your political activism. How did it get started?

My political activism started when I came out as a lesbian. Before that I was a conservative, much like my family. So, it was my sexual identity that politicized me. And, through that, I started becoming active in the US LGBT movement, locally in Connecticut, and then regionally. And, at that point, I was editing and publishing the lesbian/gay paper in Connecticut called, "Metroline." When I left that job, I was looking for something that was broader, politically and geographically. So, I had learned of this organization called Political Research Associates (PRA), a fantastic work. I was a Research Analyst there, that was the job I took after that.

What was it like becoming the Executive Director of IGLHRC?

It was an honor to be in that position for number of reasons. I was compelled to do international work because, again, for many years I really had visions and dreams of being able to do this kind of activism in Pakistan, in my home country. So, IGLHRC was for me a way, again, to broaden the ways in which I was able to do this kind of activism. It was an honor in my ways and a dream come true because I was able to go back to Pakistan and was asked to do a seminar on sexuality. And that was the first time ever in that country that that kind of discussion took place in a public space. So, that was very important to me. It was a real honor and, I think, at the same time very difficult job to have.

Because of its international aspect.

Right. Generally, the work loads. But, other than that it was a real honor and privilege because of the kind of people I was able to work with. The activists all over the world. It was huge learning experience. I think it is really important for all of us to recognize the kind of activism that happens around sexual rights and sexuality in many different ways. There is just a lot. We have so much to learn from interacting with other people.

What was the most memorable thing for you for your work with IGLHRC?

Gosh, there is so many. Again, I was probably mesmerized in terms of my interaction with activists who were doing and building grassroots movements in their home countries. In terms of personally for me, it was the moment of going to Southeast Asia, to India, to Srilanka and also, especially, to Pakistan. To be able to go to Pakistan was really great. Even though the context of that visit was to visit my family, I couldn't turn down the opportunity to lead that seminar and that was really a memorable experience.

You left IGLHRC at the end of last year, what are you doing right now and where are you headed?

Right now, I'm taking a little time off and getting some rest. We are living down here in southern California where my partner is teaching at the University of California, Irvine, which is the reason we moved down here. And, then, starting soon, I'm going to be do some consulting and getting back to some writing, which is something I miss doing in terms of all the administration. So, those are the two things I'm going to be working on.

As you are aware of it, the queer Muslim community has been organizing and establishing themselves for the past decade. What are your thoughts on how we chose to approach this? And where would you like to see the community in the future?

I think it is exciting that there is a movement around these issues. And I think where I would like to see it headed is really looking for guidance from the queer Muslims living in their home countries, because those are the people that are affected in many different ways and, sometimes, in many more difficult situations. So, I think, we have a lot to learn from that kind of leadership. I also think we need to engage in some more scholarly research, in terms of interpretations of the Qur'an, so that we are well equipped to respond to the kind of attacks we face from the fundamentalists.

What are your thoughts on same-sex marriages?

I think that is a complicated question because marriage as an institution has many flaws and I'm interested in, as a progressive activist, institutional change. And, so, I don't agree with the movement in the US, in particular, that calls for gay marriages as in we want to be like you, heterosexual. I think that there are many benefits that marriage gives to people that are important—in terms of health care, hospital visitation rights and inheritance rights—but I think we need to take the aspect of marriage that function well and take those that don't and integrate them into a broader institution where people have a choice.

I'm in a committed relationship and that is important to me. We are fortunate because of the state we live in—in terms of health-care and other issues that are available to us as a couple—but what I would like to see happen, if you take health-care, for example, is that we could each designate a person, it wouldn't have to be spouse it could be a friend or family. I think it is important for us to really conceptualize these issues more broadly and think about the institutions in terms of their flaws and benefits.

In every interview that I do, I ask this last question: if you had the power to change something about yourself, what would it be and why?

I'm really happy with the path that I'm on in terms of the person that I'm and the values in which I live my life. And when you speak about change I think I would want to continue on that path, making positive changes for myself and the people that I love, and then much more broadly in the world that I just want to continue to have some kind of impact, particularly in these times where there is calls for violence and military conflict. I want to continue as a person so that I have some impact and influence in creating a world where there is justice and peace for everybody.

<u>UPDATE:</u> Since this interview was conducted in early 2003, Surina Khan has begun working with the Ford Foundation. She is the director of the foundation's Gender Rights and Equality. Her work with the foundation focuses on Women's Rights, protection for persons with HIV/AIDS, as well as LGBT Rights.

OMAR NAHAS

Omar Nahas exemplifies the conflict between Islam and the modern world. He is a gay Muslim who refused to live in his conservative society because he wanted the type of relationship that wasn't acceptable in Syria. In Europe, he continues this type of activism with both Muslim and non-Muslim communities. He has lectured, written, and gave his views on many subjects at various places. His book, "Islam and Homosexuality" was the first of its kind in Europe from a queer Muslim. I had the chance to talk to him about his life, his work, and his vision.

You were born in Syria, did you grow up there?

Yes, I was 25 years old when I left.

What was your life like in Syria?

I had a great time there. I was born to Syrian parents, and they were both very religious. I remember being different, from a young age. I remember falling in love with my neighbor. He was about forty, and I was just ten. He did not know any thing about that. I only admired him. There was nothing sexual actually, but once I embarrassed him when I hugged him. At the time he came back from abroad.

So you remember having same-sex thoughts at early age.

Yes, I remember that far back at least. I believe I'm born like this. I think my parents knew that I am gay from other earlier experiences.

When did you yourself realize you were gay?

Actually, I thought that everybody is gay. I was surprised to realize that my brother and my uncle are not gay. It was very hard to know that I am different. I think I was 11 years old when this happened.

When did you have your first sexual encounter with other men?

I was 20 when I had my first experience. So, as you can see, I was sadly a virgin for twenty years.

Did you feel any guilt about your first experience?

Not at all. I was even surprised of my self that it was so natural and peaceful. I was complete.

When did you realize that being gay is not accepted in most Muslim communities?

I knew that at a very early age. This means I had thought a lot about it before I actually did anything. So I felt guilty way before having sex. By the time I was 20 I think I was was already sure about myself.

Sure about yourself in what way?

Sure that I am different and that I have different way of being judged by God.

How did you meet men in such a conservative country?

Honestly, it was a shock to find out that men who have sex with men and then get married were better accepted than the ones who are really gay and staying gay. So, it was not difficult to ask men if they like to have fun with me.

Did you fall in love with anyone in Syria?

Yes, I fell in love in Syria and lost my heart there. I fell in love twice there. The first one, he was also the first man I have had sex with. He was an architect, a really great person. I asked him if he would like to have a monogamous relationship with me. He said no it is not possible. Then we stayed three years together. It was a very intense relationship. We were together everyday. He slept at my home also. One day, he said that he was going to get married with a woman he knew from work. He went away. And after a month he called me and we met and talked. He asked me if I want to have sex with him, and I refused because he was then a married man. It is a sad story, and I don't really like to tell it.

What about the second one?

The second one was philosophical and was very dominant. He was having a relationship with a girl already and wanted me to get a girlfriend too. He said that he is homosexual but it is good to have a woman. We were together for two years. And one day when he went to get married with his girl, I decided to leave Syria.

Do you think they loved you?

I really think that both of my ex-es did love me very much, but they were too weak to speak up in a society like Syria.

Did you leave Syria because he got married?

I left Syria because I thought to myself "this is not going to happen for the third time to me." I wanted to be openly gay, and that was one of the best decisions I made in my life.

Where did you go after you left Syria?

I first went to Belgium, but then I decided to go directly to Holland because I did not want to stay in an Arabic ghetto in Brussels. So I went as an individual to live as an individual and discover the world.

When you came to Europe, what was your life like?

It was promising. I wanted to be free in Europe but I realized that even in Europe—when you are in a ghetto like those in Brussels—you are not really free. I left to study something I was always interested in, Islam and gay issue. So, I studied Islam and Arabic in Nijmegen-Holland. Then I went into Gay and Lesbian studies in Amsterdam.

How did you support yourself?

I worked as a translator of Arabic-Dutch.

What did you do after your studies?

I worked for a while, and then started YOESUF.

Tell me how YOESUF got started.

Queer Jihad

On February 16, 1998, I started the center [YOESUF] which was meant to bridge the gap between Islam and social issue—like Homosexuality—for the Dutch society. We wanted to spend as much time as we could on the issue of Homosexuality and Islam. So for the first three years we educated the Dutch society—Muslim and otherwise—on the issues relating to this. Then after that we did sexual diversity, not just Homosexual but everything else. In 2007, we went into Youth issues. This way we got more good people to be involved. It was a nice set up because they would have to be tolerant and open as they would otherwise not work for an organization that started its work with discussing homosexuality.

You guys published a book on Islam and Homosexuality, which you authored, correct?

Yes, it was called "Islam and Homosexuality" and it talks about the social and the religious influences in the life of a homosexual person. I started that book as an interpretation of the Qur'an, and now I think it is the most important part of the book. It talks about homosexuality and lesbianism in heaven as a part of joy in paradise. I argue in the book that when it is a part of heavenly joy it is not and cannot be a psychological disorder, because in paradise there is no disorders. Muslims have to stop calling it as such.

What would you say is the overall message of the book?

That Islam is not the problem, prejudice is and that a progressive interpretation is needed and the traditional is unjust.

I know it started with you, but what is YOESUF like today?

It is ok. We are now five permanent people (temporarily not paid), who are working fifteen volunteers and a board composed of six persons. We do not have money right now to do the job further because it grew bigger than our capacity

So what are you doing nowadays besides YOESUF?

I give trainings in Islam for teachers, social assistants, government workers and non-profit organizations. BUT I HAVE A DREAM!

What is your dream?

I want to write an integral progressive interpretation of the Qur'an, and I am looking for somebody who can adopt the project. Nothing is impossible.

Nothing is impossible. Do you think you will translate your book into English?

No. I think some other interested people may do that. I would like to give the task to the generation after me.

What do you think our community needs more than anything else?

I think queer Muslim movement needs a kind of Islamic ILGA, which coordinates all the organizational work globally.

Do you think the community is ready for something like that?

We are ready! We have to be. This would help us all so much.

How big is the queer Muslim movement in Europe?

Not that big, actually. But that can change.

Back to you, have you fallen in love since Syria?

I still have a heart, you know. Yes. I'm in love right now with a great man.

Are you two together?

We are not living together, but we are together every time we are free.

Are you happy?

I'm happy. Very happy.

What would you like to tell the young boy in Syria, or anywhere today, just realizing that he is gay?

Be yourself, love god, and he will love you without any limitations. He will even make other people love you. Being gay is a gift from God. Take care of your gift. It is better to be gay and being good to people than acting straight and being unhappy.

In every interview that I do, I ask this last question: if you had the power to change something about yourself, what would it be and why?

Better time management! Because I want to do quite a lot of things and my organizational skills are not fantastic.

<u>UPDATE:</u> Since this interview was conducted in 2004, Omar Nahas has written two other books, "Gay and Muslim" and "The Other Jihad," which cover issues relating to Islam, queer sexuality, Muslim youth, and Europe. He continues to lecture, and teach at various institutions.

EL-FAROUK KHAKI

Since the early 1990s, El-Farouk Khaki has been a pioneer. He formed the first support group for gay and lesbian Muslims in Canada. He called it *Salaam*, offering a peaceful solution to an issue that haunted many before him: how exactly do we reconcile our sexuality and our faith? Later, he would become a respected immigration attorney, defending the rights of gay and lesbian refugees in his country. And in recent years, he has run for political office. But whether he is running a campaign or leading a prayer, something that is always present in El-Farouk's life is his undying support for the equality of all people.

Something people don't imagine when they first meet you is that you were born in Tanzania.

Because to be "African" you apparently must be black. Or white. It is interesting that white people's nationalities are never questioned. A Chinese Canadian who is a fifth-generation Canadian is still asked, "Where do you come from—originally?"

I know. It is one of those things about being a minority in the West. Do you consider yourself African?

Yes. I am a queer African Muslim man of color, a feminist and an immigrant. I am brown skinned from Black Africa and was born into a small Muslim community in Tanzania that has been traditionally marginalized by the mainstream.

Do you have memories of Africa?

I was seven when we left. Yes, I have some memories. I have bits of memory—of Dar es Salaam and Nairobi, which is where my mum and I stayed after fleeing Tanzania and before we got to England. My bits include family, school, sitting on my grandmother's lap, or listening to my grandpa tell me stories. He was good at telling stories. I have bits from a trip to Bagamoyo, the old German capital of Tanzania, and going to the beach after *fajr*, as the fishermen were bringing in their catches and selling them on the spot. I recall listening to my mum on the phone with my dad, telling him to remain in London while she found a way for her and me to get out of Tanzania. I also remember going on safari with my aunt Dolly, her now late husband Mohamed Amin, and my baby cousin Salim.

Why did your family leave Africa?

My family fled Tanzania in 1971 to escape political and religious persecution. In many parts of Africa that were under British colonial rule, you had to be Christian to get an education. That is why even in majority-Muslim countries, the educated and political elite is Christian. The same was true in Tanzania, where Muslims were at least equal in number to the Christian population. My father was part of the independence movement. After independence we had "one party democracy," which means we had a dictatorship. Hence after independence, the repression of people who were potentially "problematic" for the regime. My father fit into that category, so we had to leave.

Where did your family flee to?

After we had all left Africa, we spent three years in the United Kingdom, essentially without status. Then, my parents secured permanent residence papers for Canada. We landed in Toronto in March 1974 to find two feet of snow. In Tanzania my father had been involved in the Experiment in International Living, an organization that brought Westerners to Africa and gave them homestays. The same organization set up a homestay for us in Toronto with a Jewish family. My first religious festival in Canada was attending *Purim*. For a week, I was the only Muslim attending a private Jewish school.

Would you say your family was or is religious?

Yes. My family is of mixed origins—racially, ethnically, as well as sectarian—and always devout. But the *fundo-Wahhabi-Salafi* Islam, "my way is the only Islam" way, is something that is post-petrodollars. So in my family, there was never a conflict between praying and being a modern, cosmopolitan humanist. My father did *hajj* in 1964, and *salat* is a regular feature in my home. My parents made no distinction between Muslim and non-Muslim, only good people versus not so good people. They taught me that Allah was *al-Rahman* and *al-Raheem* (the Most Gracious and the Most Compassionate) and that Islam was an inclusive, accepting, and progressive religion.

How did your family's inclusive views affect your experiences growing up?

Well, one example is from our time in England. There were few non-Christian kids at my school. Most of them had letters from their families to be excused from morning assembly where, in addition to administrative matters, the Lord's Prayer and Christian hymns were recited. My parents, however, did not want me excused. They felt that an exposure to faith was important. I loved performance and had a role in every Christmas play. My teacher, Ms. Jenkins, asked me once about my parents and the fact that they did not object to me participating in Christian plays. She was so taken by my response that Jesus was a prophet and my parents had no objections that she made a point of telling them so at the next parent-teacher meeting.

Tell me about your early life in Canada.

What about it? I was a ten-year-old fey brown boy with a heavy upper-class English accent. There were few Muslims around, and homosexuality, even in Canada, was only just becoming public and ok.

Was it easy to assimilate?

I do not consider myself assimilated. I consider myself integrated. Canadian culture is largely amorphous and undefined. It is an on-going experiment. My father was educated in England; my mother had been an English teacher back in Tanzania. English is my first language, and I spoke it with a polished English accent when we came to Canada. "The West" was not a foreign concept for us coming from British-colonized Africa. My parents' understanding of Islam is not that it is "eastern" or "western," but universal.

Queer Jihad

When did you first realize you were gay?

When I started hitting puberty—or maybe that's when it started to hit me—around age twelve, I realized that I was excited by other guys. Accepting that I was gay was a longer and harder process.

Tell me about your feelings back then about being gay and Muslim.

While open and liberal in the views and practice of Islam that my parents instilled in me, coming to terms with my emerging understanding of sexuality and my attraction for other men was a challenge for me. The story of Lot troubled—even traumatized—me. I went to bed many times over many years praying I'd wake up straight. I never did. I wrestled with how a Merciful Creator would create me this way, only to condemn me. I know this to be the experience of many LGBT Muslims and of other faiths also. I thought it was wrong. I thought I was cursed. I would pray to wake up straight. I kept praying for that many nights over the years_but kept waking up still gay.

Did you know other gay Muslims growing up?

Not really. There were very few queer people of colour back in the day, even fewer who were Muslim. There were one or two others, but we generally avoided each other. I think out of fear of being outed and for fear of being marginalized by other (white) queers.

You went to school to become a lawyer. Was that something expected of you or was it something you wanted to go into?

I started university when I was sixteen. I would have completed my bachelor's at age twenty in political science or anthropology. Fearing unemployment, I decided to continue my studies and applied to law school, figuring that a law degree would be a helpful stepping stone. I love science fiction. When I was younger, I had wanted to study genetics, but I found the academic program too restrictive, so I pursued the arts. When I was only about five, I decided I wanted to be an actor. Well, I guess, in some ways, being a lawyer is being a performer.

You are very much interested in the rights of others. Where do you think that comes from?

My commitment to social justice and human dignity is entrenched in my own experience of marginalization as "the other" due to my race, my religious identity, and the expression of my sexual orientation as a visibly queer man. My parents and their roles in the community instilled the importance of active commitment to social justice and human dignity in me.

Was that why you chose to go into immigration law?

I wanted karmicly clean work. And as I have been involved in human rights work and anti-oppression activism, in addition to my family's own experience with persecution and flight, it seemed appropriate. Plus, in doing the kind of refugee work that I do, there is overlap with anthropology, which is a passion.

Where does your interest in anthropology stem from?

I am fascinated by human culture and systems that perpetuate those cultures and norms. I guess, in part it is connected to my own search for identity and community. Understanding the interconnections between culture, belief, environment and class, gender, orientation, and race is interesting. Learning how they impact one another, and how they affect the structuring of human society is not only fascinating, but vital to human survival and growth in today's world.

You are known for your experience with gay refugee cases.

Yes. It is what I am known for; about 80% of my casework is representing refugees who are LGBTQ, women fleeing gender violence/persecution, and people living with HIV/AIDS.

Tell me a bit more about your refugee work.

In 1993, I opened up my own law firm doing refugee and immigration law, work I was very passionate about. My activism in the LGBT communities led to referrals of mostly gay and bisexual men seeking asylum on account of their sexual orientation. My clients have come from over a hundred different countries from Latin America, Africa, the Caribbean, Asia, and Eastern Europe. In many of these countries, same-sex activity and relationships are criminalized or "public morality" laws are used to target, marginalize, and persecute LGBT people. There were very few such claims in the mid-1990s, and a lot of unfamiliarity and even uncertainty in the law.

Asylum on the basis of sexual orientation or gender identity was a new area of refugee law when I began my practice. One of my earliest cases was that of Jose Ortigoza, a gay man from Venezuela, who filed for refugee protection when he was detained by Canada Immigration. His claim had an extraordinary number of sittings at the Canadian Immigration and Refugee Board (IRB)– eight in total when the average is one or two. At one of the sittings, there were over twenty-three observers from human rights NGOs including Amnesty International and others, when generally there are few observers if any. Eventually, Jose was determined to be a Convention refugee and allowed to remain in Canada. The case brought awareness to a variety of immigrant/refugee advocacy groups of the particular needs and barriers facing LGBT refugees and the need for refugee organizations to address their needs. Most refugee claims are in private. Jose's hearing, upon application by the media, was public and is listed in the Canadian Library of Parliament. It led to the IRB introducing sensitivity training on LGBT human rights issues.

Is it safe to say that your legal work reinforced your activism?

Yes. My work on behalf of my clients necessarily explores the impact of the criminalization of sodomy, and of public morality laws on the lives of LGBTQ people. It also deals with how LGBTQ people are marginalized, stigmatized, and targeted in public discourse by politicians, religious leaders, and others. I also represent all women, regardless of their sexual orientation and gender identity or expression, who fear or are fleeing gender based violence. The understanding and use of international human rights concepts and decisions is integral to my representation and advocacy of queer asylum seekers. As a result, I address issues around mental and physical health as well as barriers including homophobic, racial, and religious stereotypes that negatively impact LGBTQ immigrants and refugees. In addition, I am often called to critique and assess government policies, institutions, and legislation for differential impacts especially on women and LGBTQ people.

You started Salaam back in 1991. Tell me what led to its creation.

When I moved to Toronto in 1989, I started meeting other queer Muslims who identified as Muslim and as queer. I thought, "Yes! I am not the only one!" Some had issues with being Muslim, or gay, or both. Some seemed to want to embrace both identities. So, I founded Salaam in 1991 as part of my own search for community. Queer Muslims face persecution in many Muslim countries, and even in the West we are marginalized and stigmatized by mainstream Muslim communities. Salaam was a safe space for queer Muslims at a time when we did not have many safe spaces.

What was it like being part of a group like that?

I was pleased with the initial responses and the number of responses. It was very exciting to be doing something like that, and also a little frightening. It was pre-Internet and I had no idea who or what was out there.

Why did you dissolve the group?

I dissolved the group for a number of reasons. One included a death threat to a student newspaper that had published an article written by me and a couple of other Salaam members about being Muslim and gay. The threat was written by four cells of the Islamic Jihad operating out of four Ontario universities. While there were over one hundred people on the Salaam contact list, including folks in New York and even Washington State and California, the local folks were all concerned about their identities, their families' knowing, or being exposed. Communication was by phone.

Queer Jihad

Everyone had their specific instructions on what to say and not to say if they were called.

It was a lot of work, and while many people liked Salaam and had great ideas, people were hesitant to take on any of the work because of their own concerns and worries. Too many people thought I had all the time, all the money, and no fear or family like they did.

So after the threat, I said, "One person does not a movement make. Maybe now is not the right time." I shut down operations in 1993.

And then you reinstated the organization in the late 1990s and it is still going on.

Faisal Alam has said that he heard about Salaam and started looking for us, but we had already closed down by then. With the advent of the Internet, he put the word out—looking for other queer Muslims. Hence, the Al-Fatiha gathering in New York City in 1998. After Al-Fatiha started in New York City, a chapter was opened up in Toronto. I was only involved from afar as support for Mohammed, a young gay Muslim man who started the chapter. About two years later, we decided to go back to using Salaam as our name. We still had name recognition, so there was continuity; it was Canadian as opposed to American, and since many people thought Al-Fatiha was too religious sounding, we reclaimed the name Salaam. The group's original name was "Salaam -- a social/support group for lesbian and gay Muslims." Now we call ourselves "Salaam: Queer Muslim Community." I suggested the word "community" because it was, and continues to be, an aspiration for the creation of a network of people with a sense of belonging—something I believe to be necessary and vital for people who are often taught to hate themselves in God's name from early childhood because of their sexual orientation, gender identity or expression. I see Salaam's work as helping to end the social schizophrenia between public and private and the self-hate so prevalent among many LGBTI Muslims as a result of rejection and demonization by their cultures and societies, generally in the name of Islam and their visions of God.

Afdhere Jama

Tell me about the Salaam conference.

The conference, held in June 2003, drew more than 150 registered participants from Canada, the United States, New Zealand, England, and other places. At the gathering, on June 20, Ghazala Anwar became the first female *imam* of a public mixed-gender congregation in Canada. The participants in the prayer service included Muslims and non-Muslims, queers and straight people. Her *khutba* was about establishing *juma* services and building community. Over one hundred people participated in the prayer. My partner Guy and I prayed in the first row, a straight Iranian woman prayed between us. Though she claimed not to be a believer, she shed a tear or two during the service, as did many others in the room. The service and the deliberate choice of a female imam linked the struggles for justice on the basis of gender with the struggles for justice and dignity of LGBT people.

The issue of female imams and women's rights seems to come up repeatedly. As a gay man, why is this so important to you?

As we planned the conference, gender equality came to the forefront. I have always seen the advancement of women's equality as a struggle that parallels the one for queer human rights. I believe that homophobia and misogyny are flipsides of the same coin that is patriarchy. Many Muslim gay men don't recognize that, although they have male privilege that allows them to enter the front door of the mosque, they are loathed because they "choose" to be penetrated, and are hence like women, and ergo lesser than "real" men.

What else was special about the Salaam Conference?

A regular participant in Salaam events, David, a gay Sephardic Jewish man, had wanted to volunteer at the conference. He registered late and was told that we did not need any more volunteers. I suggested that we not turn away volunteers as some could not afford the registration fee. Less than a week before the conference, I received an email from a gay Muslim conference participant from the United Kingdom requesting an American Sign

Queer Jihad

Language (ASL) translator. Allah works in mysterious ways, as David was the only person at the conference who knew ASL.

How active is Salaam in the larger queer community?

Salaam's reach and impact has been greater than one limited to queer Muslims. We are known in the community and have worked with other communities including the 519, GLAD (Gays and Lesbians of African Descent), ASAAP (Alliance for South Asian Aids Prevention), Mirchi (queer South Asian women's group), and many others including the Inside Out Film Festival, Canadian Muslim Union, Muslims for Progressive Values, APAA (Africans in Partnership Against AIDS), and others. We are working on a potential project with Egale Canada. A number of our members and board, past and present, are also active in the larger queer communities. Our profiles add to Salaam's profile.

We have also outreached to straight Muslims and particularly women, as well as non-Muslim queers. Our support group, originally facilitated by Farzana Doctor and Suhail Alsameed, has helped many people reconcile their faith and sexual orientation. Carol Chery, a young queer woman and a Jehovah's Witness, started coming to the Salaam Support Group. As a person of faith, she had difficulty in coming to terms with her faith and her orientation. It was the Salaam support group that helped her in her journey. She remains a supporter of Salaam and regularly attends our activities including the annual Salaam/Peace Iftar with her wife, Stephanie James.

How involved are you with the Salaam organization now?

I am still on the board. We are currently in the process of revitalizing the Salaam board and have several new members. While former members have stepped away from the board, they remain involved and engaged with the group.

We all have people or events in our lives that mold us into becoming who we are. Do you have such a pivotal person or moment you could share with us?

My life journey is incomplete without mention of my first partner, Guy Lahaie, and my parents.

Guy was a Franco-Ontarian and an ex-Catholic. Having been introduced to evangelical Christianity by some family members, Guy was very spiritual but weary of organized religion and any who claimed to have exclusive title to the Truth and to being 'saved'. He helped me open up my understanding of Islam. It was Guy who first began to challenge my own gendered and cultural assumptions and biases that flavored my Islam. He helped me begin to articulate and challenge my consciousness on the exclusion of women from the position of *imam*. These unarticulated doubts combined with my own ambivalence around the story of Lot were the starting point of my quest for answers that led me to create Salaam and Min-Alaq, a nascent "progressive" Muslim group I was involved in creating and which functioned from 1991 till 1994. Those are the foundation for my ongoing work since.

Five years into our relationship, Guy was diagnosed with advanced HIV infection. Guy helped me see how lucky we were; that the glass was half full, even if it was also half empty. Despite his many struggles with his health and with medication, Guy had a zest and relish for life.

In early 2003, I was asked to organize the Salaam/Al-Fatiha conference. When I asked his opinion whether I should assume the role, citing my concern for his health and our safety, he told me that if we did not do this, who would? Guy joined Salaam's board and through this also journeyed towards his embrace of Islam.

You lost Guy only months after the Salaam conference. Can you tell me about that experience?

Guy passed away at about 3:30 a.m. on February 22, 2004 at home, in my arms, with loved ones surrounding us. Later that evening I stepped out of the house for some fresh air and space. As I looked up in the sky, I saw the perfect star and crescent. It was the first day of Muharram, the first month of the Islamic calendar and the month in which Imam Hussain was martyred. I knew that Guy was at peace.

The funeral was held on Tuesday at a local church. Our friend Raven Rowanchild and I had put together an interfaith service that

Queer Jihad

included recitations and readings from the Old and New Testaments, Psalms, the Qur'an and Sikh hymnals. Over three hundred people came to the funeral. United Church of Canada Minister Cheri di Novo officiated the service, at the end of which I led the *janaza*, the funeral prayer, within the sanctuary of the church. As always, everyone was invited to join and most people did.

My father and our friend Nur Marcus, a Sufi, led the *zikr* as we carried Guy's coffin out of the church to the crematorium where we continued to chant "La Illaha ill Allah" as I lit the flames. I felt blessed to have my parents and friends with me.

Guy's passing ended one chapter of my life. My healing came through the love of my family and friends and my certainty of God's love and divine plan. That did not make my days or nights easy. I made a conscious choice not to look for a new relationship soon after.

How has the experience of losing someone you loved so dearly to HIV/AIDS affected your life and work?

Prior to Guy's diagnosis in 1993, I was well aware of the human rights issues raised by the HIV/AIDS epidemic because of the loss of friends, and through clients who were HIV-positive gay asylum seekers. Through my relationship with Guy, however, I became exposed on a first-hand basis with HIV-related stigma and discrimination. I also experienced stigma and discrimination upon his death, as many imputed that I am HIV-positive, though by the grace of God, I am not. HIV/AIDS has profoundly impacted my life, and combating HIV/AIDS stigma and discrimination is an agenda that I have integrated into my professional and social justice work.

You also emphasized the influence of your parents.

I am indeed blessed by my parents, Gul and Aziz Khaki, and owe them much. My father has been a human rights/social justice activist all his life. I guess I get my zeal for community organizing, politics, and social justice from him. However, it is my mother who has been my support and my backbone, my friend, and my teacher.

I owe her for her determination, inner strength, courage, and her unconditional love and support for me, even when it has not always been easy for her.

Muslim parents are not known for being accepting of their gay child. Your parents are an exception. Do you engage each other on the issue of your orientation?

While my parents never rejected me because of my sexual orientation, their acceptance of it has been a process. Their humanism challenged by their traditionalism, they knew many LGBT people but would prefer their son to be straight.

I am truly thankful for my parents and their vision of Islam that they instilled in me. I am well aware that my orientation and some of my views have been a challenge to them. I'd like to think that they too have grown in their Islam and their humanity.

Tell me about your involvement with the New Democratic Party.

Running for political office was another way for me to push the envelope.

In 2007, I was awarded the Stenert-Ferreiro Award, Canada's biggest recognition of leadership in the LGBTQ community, honouring our unsung heroes who work to achieve understanding and change. At that point, I asked Allah "What do I do next?" My city councilor and former Member of Parliament were both present at the awards ceremony. It came up that the NDP were looking for a candidate to run in the by-election. The NDP is the left-of-centre party in Canada. I have been long associated with it. I made a call: I was signed up and eventually won the nomination.

I have run for federal Member of Parliament twice as a candidate with the NDP—in the March 2008 by-election and in the October 2008 federal election. Had I been elected, I would have been the first queer Muslim to be elected to a federal parliament.

How did being Muslim and gay affect your candidacy, do you think?

Queer Jihad

Well, among other things, in trying to solicit support, I spoke to another NDP candidate who is Bengali and asked him to help me form some connection with the 5000-plus Bengalis who live in my riding (electoral area). He informed me that they had refused to support me because I was openly gay. The perverse truth is that they had no problem supporting openly gay candidates that were not Muslim. The City Councilor and Member of provincial parliament were both openly gay men who were married to their partners. Yet, despite my work and positioning on immigration, housing, homelessness and other issues, some of the Muslims in my riding rejected me because I was Muslim and gay. Pathetic is the word that comes to mind. After my second campaign, I was happy to fade out of the political limelight. At least for now.

Tell me about your current relationship.

I have been in this relationship for four years. My partner, Troy Jackson, is "black Scotian" of mixed African, Native, and European descent. He is a truly lovely human being, and I am thankful to have him in my life. By day, he manages my law firm. He is also a singer. A video for his single, "The Batty Boys Revenge," addresses the issue of homophobia and violence against queers.

Troy uses singing and song-writing as a means of social change and consciousness raising. Muslims often say that Allah loves beauty. Troy helped bring beauty into my life through his music and his heart.

Troy embraced Islam at some undefined moment after we started dating. His choice. I had simply told him at the beginning that I was Muslim and that this was important to me. I asked him to participate with me in the important events and occasions, as I was willing to do so with him for what he felt was important.

We have just come back from doing *umrah* with my parents, aunt Dolly and cousin Salim. It was an amazing experience. We have made the *niyat* to go again, *Insha'Allah*.

In 2009, Troy and I co-founded "Human+," a project dedicated to exploring the intersectionalities of our common humanity. Also in 2009, we co-founded with Dr. Laury Silvers the "el-Tawhid Juma Circle"—a queer- and woman-positive egalitarian and inclusive Muslim Friday prayer space. We have now been functioning on a weekly basis for twenty-four months. Since then, two other "el-Tawhid" communities have formed in Washington D.C. and Atlanta, Georgia. We are currently networking with people in Canada, the United States, the United Kingdom, South Africa and other places to begin similar spaces. We hope this endeavor, along with other existing inclusive prayer spaces in Los Angeles and New York City, will revolutionize many Muslim communities.

You mentioned going to *umrah* recently with Troy, your parents, and other close relatives. Do you care to share some of your impressions with us?

It is hard to describe. For those that know me, that's saying a lot! I was awed. Transformed. It was a spiritually and visually breathtaking experience. I think we all cried at the first sight of the Ka'aba. There were so many contrasts and paradoxes. We were painfully aware that we had to be careful and "discreet." Despite all the issues, to be in prayer with 800,000 people in close proximity was truly stunning. There were many highlights, but the ones I will cherish the most are the hours I spent at the Ka'aba in prayer and conversation with my partner and my family, and especially our last prayer in Mecca where I stood in *salat* with my mother and aunt, my father and my partner— together in the Ka'aba, something we sadly cannot do in other mosques around the world, not even in Medina.

You and Troy have done so much together. Now that gay marriage is legal in Canada, would you ever get married?

Yes. I would want to have a *nikah*. Troy and I are also about to start the process of adoption as we would like to have kids. I told Troy that he will have to decide when he is ready and ask me. I'm waiting.

So what should we expect from you next?

Queer Jihad

As part of my spiritual journey and growth, I formally joined a Rifai Sufi community last year in 2010. In addition to performing *umrah*, I also attended the al-Jama'a LGBT Retreat just outside Philadelphia. Another amazing and transformative experience. Currently, I am organizing "al-Inshirah – An Expansion of the Heart: Building for Tomorrow" Salaam Outgames Human Rights conference that will take place in Vancouver in July 2011.

This year, I have been asked to be part of the "Envisioning Global LGBT Human Rights" Project, which examines British-inherited sodomy laws and the responses by queer activists and movements. The project aims to look at India and South Africa, as well as several countries in British East Africa and the Caribbean. India and South Africa serve as points of reference where sodomy laws have been successfully overturned and where queer communities and activists face ongoing challenges in creating accepting societies. As part of this project, I recently visited Kenya, Zanzibar, Botswana, and South Africa, where the team and I met with a variety of queer and other human rights groups and organizations.

I'd like to have a television show that explores progressive and creative thought, people and issues. As I said before, I have wanted to be an actor since I was five years old. I'd love to host a show that is a critical and intersectional exploration of society and the rich tapestry that is human culture as manifested by people and groups around the globe today.

And what would you say to those inspired by your story?

There remains much work to be done to create, nurture and foster inclusive *tawhidic* Muslim spaces where diversity and inclusivity are celebrated, not just given lip service. The inherent dignity of every human being regardless of gender, gender identity, orientation, race, linguistic group, dis/ability or class must be recognized as Allah-given and exemplified by the Qur'anic declaration that Allah is closer to each one of us than our own jugular vein. While there are existing and emerging groups and communities, our challenge remains to spread the word and connect the voices into a world-transforming force. *Insha'Allah*.

Afdhere Jama

In every interview that I do, I ask this last question: if you had the power to change something about yourself, what would it be and why?

I can be easily annoyed and irritated by people. I pray for more patience.

<u>NOTE:</u> This interview was originally conducted years ago, but it has since been updated recently as it was included in the "Progressive Muslims Identities," a collection of stories from the progressive Muslim community in North America edited by Ani Zonneveld, Vanessa Karam, and Olivia Samad.

FAISAL ALAM

It was late Spring in 1999 when a *New York Times* article created a buzz in many Muslim circles in the United States and around the world. The article had covered a local conference on being gay and Muslim, organized by a newly formed support group called "Al-Fatiha Foundation," which had been registered in New York City just four months earlier. It was from that article that I first heard about Faisal Alam, the founder of *Al-Fatiha*. Three years later, on a humid August night in downtown Minneapolis, I would have the chance to talk to him about his life.

Tell me about your early childhood?

I was born in Germany in 1977, and we lived there for about six years. Then we moved to Saudi Arabia, and we were there for about four years. After that we moved to Pakistan, and we lived there for about a year. And then, in 1987, we moved to a small town in Connecticut, and I have been in the United States ever since.

When did you come out to yourself?

I think it is typical in the sense that I always knew that I was different, that I was attracted to guys, but I didn't know that that was not normal. I knew that it was something weird, something different, and I didn't put word to it until probably I met my first boyfriend at age sixteen.

What were your thoughts about being gay?

I knew that it was wrong—that is what I was taught for my whole life—but I didn't know if I could change that or anything. I mean, I didn't know what to do with it. All I knew was that it was really weird because when we were together it was really amazing. He was such a beautiful person. He loved me a lot. He took care of me and we had amazing nights, because we used to spend a lot of time in his house. But then when I came home in the morning, I had this immense guilt of what I had done the night before.

Queer Jihad

What are your thoughts on being queer now?

I think we are born queer. I don't believe in all this gay gene or whatever, but I do think our desires are natural and that they are God-given. So, yes, definitely I think that God creates queer people and straight people. With certain people, queer people can become straight, straight people can become queer. I think that sexuality is fluid, and I don't think it's a matter of a choice, necessarily, but certain people can choose different things. That doesn't mean you can just turn straight or turn gay—because your natural inclinations are already there.

One thing I have heard from a lot of queer Muslims is that they blamed God for creating them that way. Has that ever happened to you?

Yes, I think so. I thought that for a long time. It is interesting because, on one hand, we ask God for help because we want Him to change us. On the other hand, we get upset at Him because He is not changing us. He created us this way, and when prayer are not answered you ask, "Why are you making me go through this?" But I think that—and I think to some extent I still feel that—I got angry at God often. It's human nature to question God for why He created us, to ask Him what is in this place that He wants from us, like all of these, you know, different emotions that we have. But, ultimately, I think we all have to understand that life is a test. This is what in Islam we are taught; that our existence is a test. In many ways, our sexuality is our test to see if in the end we will still believe in Him and overcome the obstacles of faith.

What was college life for you like in Boston?

When I got to Northeastern, I was deeply closeted and I was also engaged to a woman at the time. I was immediately recruited into the Islamic Society of Northeastern University. So, for at least a year, it was very difficult because I was in denial about my sexuality. I thought that if I got married to this girl, everything would be okay. But then she broke off the engagement.

Was it an arranged marriage?

It wasn't an arranged marriage. She was someone that I liked and she liked me. And there is a whole another complicated story on how it happened.

Were you in love with her?

I was. I think that I was attracted to her emotionally and spiritually. I have always believed that there are different levels of attraction. A physical attraction is one level and you can definitely be attracted to people mentally, spiritually, emotionally. I had all that with her.

Was she a Pakistani?

Yes. She grew up in the US and she was a few years younger than I was. She is married now and she has kids with another person.

Why did she brake off the engagement?

She prayed to Allah during Ramadan and she asked, "Is this right for me to do?" And the inclination that she got from Allah was that something was wrong, and that it wasn't going to work out. Looking back upon it, obviously the reason that it wasn't going to work was because the person she was about to marry was queer, you know. And I didn't know that until six months later. I think that Allah was looking out for both of us. What is fascinating about the story though is that when she broke off the engagement, her parents were upset that she broke off the engagement, trying to convince me that they were going to convince her to re-engage with me. And I said to them, "It is her decision." I really strongly believe that. Of course, six months later I exploded out of the closet.

What was your family's reaction to your coming out?

My mother's reaction was worse than I expected it to be. I thought my dad would be more upset than my mother was. My mother was not happy, I mean she has been through so many of the things that parents go through. She has been through denial, intolerance, semi-acceptance—all the phases that parents go through. She is been back and forth, and she even rejected me for a

Queer Jihad

while, which was hard for me because I was very close to my mother.

What led to "Al-Fatiha"?

I thought I couldn't be the only one that was going through this, because even though I knew my first boyfriend was Muslim, he converted to Islam and it wasn't the same. I needed to find someone like who was born into Islam. Someone who looked like me. Someone, you know, who grew up in the same environment. Someone you can relate to. Because, at first, I really thought I was the only born Muslim who was facing these issues, who struggled with being gay and Muslim.

I went online and I did what many gay youth in this day and age do. I looked for resources for gay Muslims. What I came across was virtually nothing. I found resources for people who came from specific ethnic groups. Like there were groups for gay Arabs, gay Asians, gay Malaysians, gay Indonesians, everyone. And then there were groups for other religions. There were gay Buddhists and gay Christians, like every denomination of Christianity.

There were support groups that were online discussion groups, so I was subscribed to a queer Arab list at the time and basically I e-mailed the owner, the moderator of the group, and I said, you know, how do I start my own list. He showed me how. And so I created this list online. And, then, of course, the dilemma was, "How do I go about advertising it?" So, basically—and I guess it was naive of me to use my real name—I sent e-mail to all of these Muslim Student Association (MSA) listservs I was subscribed to, a sarcastic e-mail that said, "Oh my God, can you believe this list has started?!" And then basically I talked about the list, the purpose of the list, the fact that this is about reconciling these two identities. And then I basically told them how to join the list.

I sent out this message and it sounded like I just ran across this information somewhere else. That it wasn't really me who had done it. And I sent it to Muslim Student Association lists throughout the US, UK, Canada, and I think even Japan and Australia. I researched the e-mail addresses and I sent the message to these thousands of students throughout the world at the same time. And within minutes of sending this message out, people have started subscribing to the list. And within 48 hours, there were around 30-40 people subscribed. Because for the first time, there was this forum that has been created for people to talk about being gay and Muslim. But, at the same time, there was so much fear in the community that almost six to eight months I was the only person posting on the list.

I was like pouring out my heart and soul. Basically telling them my whole life story. I was like, "This is what Allah (SWT) says," "This is my interpretation of the Lut [Lot] story." Basically everything that my first boyfriend had taught me. Like, you know, "God created you, why would He hate you for what He created you as?" And "Why would He punish you for something you naturally are?" And "How can love be wrong, no matter whose it is, no matter what the person's gender or sex is?" But I was the only one for months.

So what did you call the list?

It was just called "Gay Muslims." It still exists.

Did people ever start talking to you?

Yes! Well, first when finally people started talking, two things happened. One thing happened that the list was infiltrated and we had to shut down the list. Because I was using my real name I was outed to the community. I was still involved with Muslim Student Association (MSA). I was still involved with Islamic Society of North America (ISNA). I was still involved with Northeastern, and many more. I was asked to leave from several of these organizations because of this issue.

Did they know you were gay?

No, they didn't know I was gay, but just the fact that I was public figure and that my views on homosexuality were so extreme, I could no longer be part of their institutions.

How was that for you?

Queer Jihad

That was really traumatic for me, because I was literally stripped away from my identity. I was very active in the community at that time. My argument was, "Just because I believe this, you are going to kick me out? You don't even know that I am gay." I also realized from these conversations—and these were the leaders of the Muslim community in the United States—that each of them had a different perspective on Islam and homosexuality.

There was no unanimity. They all agreed that it was *haram*, but they didn't know what the cause was, they didn't know what the treatment was, and they didn't know what the punishment was. It was the first time that it clicked in my head, "My God, we so don't know what's going on in this issue." Yet, we're telling the whole world that it is wrong to be gay and Muslim.

So what was the second thing that happened in the list?

The second thing was that people finally started talking and we wanted to meet. We wanted to meet in person. The first meeting happened in March of 1998 when a group of five of us came together in Washington, DC. It was the first time that I met a gay Muslim live in person. It was so amazing.

Gay Muslim with Muslim background.

Yes, with Muslim background. I met two transgendered Muslims. I was blown away. Just the five of us, we just hanged out. We talked, we went to the zoo, we went to the aquarium, we went to the museum, you know.

I was living in Boston, but we flew down to DC. When I went back to Boston, I realized there were so many issues we needed to discuss that we needed something like a retreat. So, what started off as the second American gathering became the First International Retreat for LGBT Muslims. We announced the conference, I remember it was over Columbus day weekend in 1998. Forty people came together from six different countries, from US, UK, Canada, Belgium, the Netherlands, and South Africa. And we ranged from a 15-year-old Egyptian-American cross-trainer to a 55-year-old white American who converted at the end of the retreat because he was so moved by the discussions we were having. And the only reason he came was because his boyfriend was Muslim and they were having problems in their relationship. He came with a very anti-Islamic point of view. He came to prove his boyfriend wrong. He wanted to show him that he could not be gay and Muslim. And he was so moved by the three days of intense conversations that at the last day he stood up—and I remember as soon as he stood up I had shivers down my spine because I knew what he was going to do—and he said, "I have something to tell all of you" and he took the *shahadah* in front of us all.

What an amazing story.

A queer Muslim gathering, of all places! But in those three days we talked about everything. We laughed. We had tons of translations of the Qur'an. The theme of the retreat was *Al-Fatiha*. We needed a theme, right? So I opened the Qur'an and the first thing I saw was the first chapter, Al-Fatiha. It was so appropriate. Of course, at the time, we thought that this was the first ever gathering. We later learned there were others. After three days of intense discussions and debates, at the last day we agreed that we needed to form an organization to address these issues facing our community; being gay and Muslim, and everything that comes with it. And, so, we decided to name the organization *Al-Fatiha*.

What was it like when your first photo was published?

Scary! In 2000, the *Washington Post* published my picture. This was the first time my picture was published in a major newspaper. The night before the article was published, I called up the writer and said, "I don't want my picture published."

Well, you know, it took me about three months to write the article with her. I was okay with the whole article, you know, and everything was fine.

She said, "No, Faisal, we need to have a personal face attached to it." And then she goes to say, "Oh, it is not even that big. It is a small photograph and the angle is like kinda looking up at you. You can't really tell it is you."

This photo comes out, right, and it is small but what ended up happening was that the article got syndicated and got picked up by

Queer Jihad

six other major newspapers. And the next week, my friend from San Francisco calls me and says, "Faisal, do you know that you are on the front page of the Sunday religion section and that there is a six-by-six inch photograph of you?" And I was like "What?!!!"

This was the *San Francisco Chronicle* and I was like, "Holy Shit!" And then the *Dallas Times*. And in Long Island and Chicago's major newspapers picked it up also.

And I wrote her. I wrote her an e-mail and said, "You told me..." and I said, "Do you understand that my life could be threaten because of this?"

I guess there was nothing she could do because it was the editor who got it syndicated. So, yes, I do worry. I think I freaked out when *Al-Hayyat* came out. Oh, my God, that was the worst. "Perverts Of the World Unite," that was the title and then the photo of Faisal Alam underneath it. The caption read, "Faisal Alam, the Malaysian founder and director of Al-Fatiha." Yeah, they thought I was Malaysian.

If you died today what would you want the world to know about you?

That I was a good person, that I cared about people and that I loved people. That I was this crazy queer radical Muslim that they knew and that they were fond of. I think that is what I want the people to remember me by.

Do you have any regrets?

Yes and no. I do regret certain things that I have done in my life, but then I do believe that everything you do has a purpose and a reason behind it. So, even though I may regret certain things, there were reasons for them.

What is your greatest fear?

Dying. Yes, I fear death the most. I'm just afraid of meeting Allah because there is a big piece of my heart that believes what I'm doing may be wrong.

That is so human. Sulayman X wrote about similar thing. He said that if all this [Queer Jihad website and forum] is wrong, then he is simply wrong in sincere. I think that matters to God, don't you think?

I know that in my heart, and that is what I say to people. If God in the Day of Judgment will say to me, "Faisal, Why did you this? Why did you start Al-Fatiha? Why have you led all these people astray?" I know what my answer is going to be, but I don't know how I'm going to say it.

What would be your answer?

My answer to Him would be, "I did this for you." I would say, "Because in my heart and head I felt that you wanted me to do this. And I also did this to help people. And if that is wrong, then send me to hell."

In every interview that I do, I ask this last question: if you had the power to change something about yourself, what would it be and why?

You ask that everyone? God, this question is really going to show my insecurities. Well, I would change my whole life. I would become totally different person. I would want someone else to become Faisal Alam.

UPDATE: Since this interview was originally published, Faisal Alam has resigned from *Al-Fatiha* and the organization had since closed down. He focuses on his "Hidden Voices" lectures, a series in campuses all over the United States. He currently lives in Atlanta.

ARSHAM PARSI

For some years, a group of queer Iranians have been exchanging information and supporting each other. From inside and outside of their homeland, they have committed themselves to changing their community's conservative attitude to queer sexuality and the government's harsh laws against them. This group is called the "Persian Gay and Lesbian Organization," or PGLO. In recent times, one of their members has become the face of the group, as he embodies much of their concern. His name is Arsham Parsi. He is a sweet, gentle man with a lot of heart and genuine concern for his people, the queer community, and the world at large. Here is some of the conversation I have had with him.

Where were you born?

I was born in Shiraz.

When did you first realize you were gay?

When I was about eight or nine years old.

How did you feel about it?

I felt that I was different from other boys because I loved boys. I started to think I had a problem because in Islamic culture homosexuality is not normal. You know, I have heard that God does not like someone that has sex with someone of their same sex. I started to believe that I was a sinner and began to become more religious. It was terrible, but at least I understood my feelings.

Is there any incident that stands out for you in your early life where someone had negatively responded to your sexuality?

Yes, when I was younger I had sex with my cousin. My mother found out about it, and she spoke to me too much about it and said to me many painful things.

How did that affect you?

Queer Jihad

Although I did not stop my sexual relationship with my cousin, every time we did something I felt that I had to stop but I just could not.

When did you realize that there were others like yourself out there?

Much later, I connected to the Internet and I searched on Google. It was so good because I found many people on the net that were similar to me. I was very happy because I felt that I was not alone in the world anymore.

Did you have a boyfriend in Iran?

No, I did not. As an adult I did not have any time for my personal life since I had been in LGBT rights for many years.

Why did you want to help other gays so much?

After I found out that I was not abnormal, I began to think about other gays and their hardships. I could understand because I was there myself and had bad experiences, and I wanted them to have a better life, and I told myself I have to do something. But I didn't know what to do.

So how did PGLO come about?

First, I started a small e-mail group. It was simply named "Rainbow." This was back in 2001. We would just send letters to each other, and sometimes some articles. A few years later, we made a website called "Gay Persian Boy." Anyway, the group had gotten stronger and in 2004 we changed the group to PGLO or the Persian Gay & Lesbian Organization. One of our members registered this organization in Norway, and we started our official activities. And, now I'm going to re-register it in Canada.

So, tell me who else is supporting you with this activism?

Well, we have a few people. Saba Rawi, in the Netherlands, who is our Human Rights Secretary and is also director of PGLO's branch in that country. Shahrokh Reisi, in Germany, who is our Cultural Secretary and also director in that country. Then there is Pooya, our Financial Secretary. Saghi is one of the editors of

Cheragh, our magazine. We have Mani, our Health Secretary. And Pirooz, our Social Secretary. We also have many LGBTs helping us in various positions.

Unfortunately, homosexuality is taboo in Iran and therefore many organizations and groups can not support us because if they support us they will lose their supporters. Shirin Ebadi, for example, told us she cannot support us in public. Why? Because she could not, as people don't have enough information about LGBT issues. So we have to inform them first, and then they can support us.

A lot of queer activists in Iran says they have been targeted by the government. I have heard that there was a death warrant against you. Is this true?

Yes, but I really cannot get into the details. I have had many problems but I just can't talk about it right now. My family still lives in Iran.

I understand that. Let me ask you this; the underground gay magazine MAHA has recently come out and said that they believe Ayaz and Mahmoud, who got executed last year, were killed for being gay. What do your own sources in Iran say? What does your group believe about this case?

First of all, I have to mention that MAHA is not a magazine inside of Iran. Some people said they are inside Iran but MAHA is actually from the United Kingdom. They have a few collaborators in Iran. I know them and appreciate their work, especially their two editors-in-chief in Iran. However, I don't know how they can announce the two boys were gay and executed for being gay because we didn't know those boys before their execution. Nobody heard of their names before.

Did the PGLO research about them?

No, PGLO did not research about these teens. We have a representative in Mashhad. We did call him to research about this issue, but he could not. His life was getting in danger and we preferred to stop this project as we don't want to make another tragedy.

Queer Jihad

Do you think MAHA researched about them?

I'm sure MAHA received some mails from its members, but it is not strong reason to announce for sure. We have received many e-mails from our members about this case, but they did not have documents to prove.

What do you want people to know generally about Iran?

Iranian society is so easy going. Sometimes I read news about Iran that show people as wild and criminal people. This is not true at all. Iranian people are so peaceful, and are cultured.

What problems do queer Iranians face?

Queer Iranians have two big problems: Islamic law of punishment and lack of information in society. The Iranian society doesn't support queers because they don't know who we are. They have to be informed. After that, they surely will support us. Law of punishment is a well-founded fear for queer. There are many fears. If they arrest us, what will happen? What should we do? What about our family, what should we do if they found out about our sexual orientation? And other hundreds of dark questions. If we are arrested, our family won't support us. We then face the condemnation of the law and that of our family.

Are there differences in different cities, in terms of queer life?

Definitely, big cities are better than small towns. We have many reports from the east and west of Iran. They are in the worst situations because they are more religious and therefore more homophobic.

How is the Internet changing that?

Well, they have less Internet access. But then most Iranians on the Internet really just check e-mails only. They don't do research as most of the websites are blocked.

I hear about a lot of queer Iranians seeking asylum in the West, especially in Europe. Are people always trying to leave the country?

Most Iranian queers would like to leave Iran to Europe or North America. But what they don't realize is that our problem will not be solved by immigration. I left Iran, for example, for my activities. I live in Toronto now, but unfortunately even the Iranians here are not informed about the LGBT issues. However, it is hard to tell people to stay. We tell our members to stay and try to change the society as this is more important, but unfortunately sometimes if they stay they get arrested.

How has your life changed since you came to Canada?

Wow. A lot of changes. I can now do activism without fear. I taste freedom here. I thought I was free in Iran, but now I don't think I was. I'm very happy that I can live in this country because I can now work to defend our LGBT community. Of course, homophobic people live all around the world. But if someone attacks me here I can call the police, and I'm sure the police will support me. I could not call the police when I was in Iran because the police will arrest me and not the homophobic person.

What about your love life, are you meeting guys?

I don't meet guys here because I don't have any free time for dating. I'm working about twenty hours a day.

That is a long day. Why so much work?

Because we have time differences between Toronto and Iran, and I have to work with our representatives inside Iran. So I can't go to bed sometimes before 5:00 A.M. Also, I work with the queer community in Toronto and I do this during the week. But on the weekends, it is not a weekend in Iran so I still work. I don't even have any day off.

That must be physically draining. How do you do it?

Well, I love my job. This is voluntary work and I don't receive any money from PGLO because we really don't have money. But when I help LGBT people in Iran, I feel joyful. We answer about one hundred to one hundred and fifty e-mails a day. And these people look forward to our responses, as they don't have anyone else to ask or listen to their problems. So I feel like if we don't who will?

What is the gay Iranian community like in Toronto?

Our queer community in Toronto unfortunately lives in the closet, just same as those who live in Iran, because they live in Iranian communities here and feel they cannot be out. We called the queer Iranians here to the July 19th protests but nobody joined us. They are afraid.

Do you think you will ever go back to Iran?

Yes. On Friday March 4th, 2005, at 1:30 P.M., when I escaped from Iran to Turkey, I cried heavily as I passed the Iranian border for Iran and for our LGBT situation in our country. And I made the promise to myself—and also to my homeland—that I will come back one day. I don't know when or how, but I know I want to go back one day and live there freely. I don't want to die in any other country. I will go back to Iran when we have rights. I'm in exile now and I don't have too much personal life as I'm fighting to live freely in Iran tomorrow.

How long were you in Turkey?

From March, 2005 to May, 2006. So, thirteen months.

Did you try to get into other countries before you came to Canada?

Well, not really. I applied for a UK visa on 2002. Some of my heterosexual friends and I decided to go there for business about fashion, but we didn't get the visas. Also, the UNHCR chose Canada for me. I did not really choose because I didn't have much information about different countries, but I'm so happy with their decision. I'm grateful for Canada and all that it has done for me.

How is your case status in Canada now?

I had an interview with a Canadian Immigration officer in Ankara [Turkey] on September 26th, 2005. On that day they approved my case. I came here in May, 2006, as an immigrant. I was afforded permanent residence and I can apply for citizenship in two years.

So, what should we expect from you next?

Well, in October I'll be speaking in Geneva. I'm very happy because after many years of silence we can now speak at the United Nations. On December 9th, we are planning on releasing reports on Human Rights in Iran. As for myself, I'm also planning on publishing my life story in a book in Persian and English. We are registering PGLO in Canada.

A lot of good work. In every interview that I do, I ask this last question: if you had the power to change something about yourself, what would it be and why?

I have not thought about this, because usually growing up I could do anything that I wanted. I had not been disappointed or unhappy in my childhood. I would certainly not change anything about my life now. However, I would have tried to start my advocacy a lot earlier and to help and to try stop all the murders and suicides of LGBTs in my country.

UPDATE: Since this interview was conducted in 2007, Arsham and his organization have been awarded the IGLHRC Felipa de Souza Award, Pride Toronto Award for Excellence in Human Rights, and was a main subject in Parvez Sharma's "A Jihad for Love" documentary. He has also become a citizen of Canada.

SCOTT "SIRAJ" KUGLE

I met Siraj many years ago on the Internet. Later, I would meet him at an LGBT Muslim gathering in Los Angeles. I remember we had an intense discussion about scholars and Islam, sexuality in the faith, and what has been the response on both sides. Even then one could hear in him the scholar that he is today, there was something original about his thinking. His book "Homosexuality in Islam" tells us that Siraj is still original.

What's the story behind your chosen name?

Siraj in Arabic means "a light." That is, *nur* is the light itself, and *siraj* is a source of light. The Quran uses the word *siraj* to describe the sun, as in Surat al-Furqan 25:61, when it says, "Blessed be the One who made in the heavens stellar constellations and made in them a sun and moon giving light." I always loved that *ayat* and how it uses the word *siraj*. And the Quran also calls the Prophet Muhammad by the praise-name "siraj muneer," meaning a light that gives illumination for others, as in Surat al-Ahzab 33:46.

When I became Muslim I adopted the name Siraj al-Haqq, or "the Light of Truth" with al-Haqq "the Truth" being one of the many names of God. It is a very difficult name to live up to! But it is also a noble ideal, and it reminds me of who I should be even if I don't always live up to the idea—I should be a light of truth and a reflection of the true one who gives light to others.

There is not much of a story to this, my chosen name. At first, I felt that I should not choose a name for myself. I acknowledged Islam when I was about 26 years old, after a long period of learning and growth. At that time I was studying Arabic in depth while living in Morocco, during the course of doing a PhD in Islamic Studies in the USA. I had a very dear Arab friend and the love between us was very great, so naturally I turned to him and asked him to give me a Muslim name. Without any hesitation he said, "You should be Zain al-`Abideen!"

I paused for a moment.

Queer Jihad

One problem with me is that I think too much, and every little thing that comes my way I have to analyze and ponder before I accept it. That is good in some ways, I suppose, and also bad. Now my heart didn't accept Zain al-`Abideen, so my mind was turning the name over and over to understand it.

I asked my friend, "Why do you think I should be Zain al-`Abideen?"

He said, "It was the name of the Prophet's great-grandson" and sure enough, it was the popular name of one son of Hussain, the revered grandson of the Prophet who was martyred at Karbala. That was true, but would my American mother be able to pronounce Zain al-`Abideen? Especially with its `ain sound that is tough for foreigners to say? Shouldn't I have a name that is more simple and universal? I thought all this out, and considered it for a day, and then told my beloved friend that, sorry, I can't be Zain al-`Abideen.

A few days later, I was having dinner with a friend's family who are Sayyids. At the dinner table was one daughter of the family. She was very studious, with thick glasses and a serious demeanor. She got into a deep conversation with me about religion and conversion and what it all meant. She asked me what was my Muslim name, and I was almost embarrassed to tell her that I didn't really have one yet! But I trusted her for some reason, and told her my plight of having been given a name that I could not accept.

She asked what name appealed to my heart, and I answered "Siraj." She instantly quoted the ayat of the Quran from above about God's making in the heavens a sun and a moon giving illumination. That's a good name, she said, you can be Siraj al-Din, meaning "light of the faith."

I told her that I didn't really want a name ending in al-Din, because it was limited to only one faith but the sun gave a light that was common to all faiths and all people.

She smiled and said, "Then be Siraj al-Haqq! There is nothing more universal than al-Haqq."

Instantly, my heart accepted that from her. I could be simply Siraj for people who need a simple name, and I could be Siraj al-Haqq for people who know Arabic and Islamic names. I never regretted taking this name. It inspires me when I'm feeling low.

That is a very nice story. What's your background?

I was born near Philadelphia, not far from where my parents were born in small towns in the farm country of Pennsylvania. My ancestors were mainly German immigrants who were laborers or farm workers, though there were some Scottish and English ancestors married in, who seem to have been teachers. My mother was a teacher, and her mother's mother was a teacher, so I think I got some urge from that side of the family to write and teach. My father worked hard to get an education, and he was the first in his family to excel in a profession.

His professional advancement made our family to move, first to Philadelphia and then to Honolulu. I moved to Honolulu when I was six years old, and that is where I grew up. So I really consider myself from Hawaii, though we always keep close to our roots in small town Pennsylvania where my grandparents and other extended family lived.

What was it like growing up in Hawaii?

Honolulu is a unique place to grow up. Maybe that's why there is the sun in my Islamic name! I grew up in a very American household but in an environment that was really more Asian than American. Now that Obama is president, people have a better sense of how Hawaii is unique in this way. It is a very isolated and special place, being islands in the middle of the Pacific, but it is also very cosmopolitan in its own way.

Were you raised in any particular faith?

My family was Protestant Christian, and I was raised going to Church and Sunday school, learning the Biblical stories, admiring the classical and choral music that the churches sponsored. My family emphasized that religion was really about ethics and caring interpersonal relations more than about dogma or ritual. They gave me the freedom to inquire into beliefs and make my own judgments.

In middle school we were given the option of learning a new language, and Japanese and Chinese were on offer—and were more popular!—along with the more conventional Spanish French or German. There were Buddhist pagodas, Shinto shrines, native Hawaiian temples and of course all kinds of churches. So religion for me was never about closed borders but rather about open invitations. I found out later, after moving to the East Coast for university and graduate school, just how much growing up in Hawaii affected me. I felt more akin to Asian ways of eating and being than to typically white American ways—I grimace to even say that phrase which is such a generalization. And I guess I've been struggling ever since to find a balance between them.

When did you first realize you were gay?

There is no such thing as a first realization. I feel that sexuality is something that "unfolds" in one's life, like a bud that unfolds into a flower. It was always there but not always recognizable, like a flower is there in a bud, like a bud is there in a stem. That said, I think I always realized I was "different" from other boys long before I could identify that difference with issues of sexuality. I always knew, for instance, that I would never father children—even when I was very young, maybe 7 years old. I used to know that for certain, by intuition and gut feeling. I didn't know why this would be my truth, but it was.

Were you social as a child?

Looking back at myself as child, I realize that I had difficulty socializing with most other boys—I was forced to play team sports in school and after school, but I resented it and would rather have been drawing pictures, writing stories, or playing music. I was introverted but also creative, and I took refuge in the arts and in studies. That won me some recognition and respect from parents and peers. It also kept issues of sexuality quiet and hidden while I was a teenager. I was too busy being a nerd. My sense of adventure was directed toward art, my sense of excitement was from discoveries of the mind, and my great romance was with books.

What about any love interests at school?

In school, I had no romantic encounters. Didn't miss them at all! I had a dear female friend who, looking back on it, was probably in love with me. I didn't perceive that until she asked me to be her date to the prom. I accepted because I had to, not because I wanted to—but I then began to realize how I didn't fit into the grand social narrative of heterosexual life. That was at age seventeen. How could I have been so clueless, you ask (and I ask too!). Of course, I turned to books to sort it all out. Reading and writing was my passion, and in books I saw reflections of myself more accurate than any image in a mirror.

Any books that stand out?

I remember a dawning of insight when I was reading the stories of Yukio Mishima, the great Japanese novelist. His novel "Confessions of a Mask" was about his own growing up homosexual in Japan, and suddenly I realized that all of my feelings of being "different" were exactly like his, and that his situation was my situation. Pieces of the puzzle began to fall into place, and the images, scents, urges and passions of sexuality began to acquire a form and name in my mind. My heart was far behind, you see! But my mind was leading the way down a path that I didn't realize was dangerous. I was delightfully naïve.

The state of innocence. What came after that?

In that state, I left my family to attend university far away. There I fell in love with a man for the first time, a fellow student and dear friend. That love was rewarding but it was not reciprocated and it never took expression in physical intimacy. It did give me, however, an irrefutable self-knowledge that I was gay and that only in homosexual love could I find fulfillment. But fulfillment was still far away. For me, acknowledging being homosexual was not about sex, and it was clear to me that this is who I am before I ever had sexual intimacy with a man.

Queer Jihad

Realizing that this path was difficult if not dangerous, and that I would be rejecting much of what my family expected from me, I decided that it was safer to romance a woman. Brilliant, right? But I was so fortunate to have many powerful, beautiful and spiritually glowing women in my life as friends. One of them was my schoolmate in Honolulu, and returning from university she and I tried out a romance. It was beautiful in many ways, and she taught me many things about loyalty, love, and life. But as a heterosexual romance, we failed because, I realized slowly, I was not heterosexual and was very bad at pretending. She realized it, too. And she had the guts to tell me what I was only beginning to admit to myself. And so I'm always grateful to her for being so compassionate with me.

Let's talk about your introduction to Islam.

I suppose that my only girlfriend was also my first Muslim friend. She gifted me my first Quran, a Penguin edition paperback translation into English, which I still have and cherish. The Quran didn't really flash in my eyes with a blinding light, but it glimmered. I read it in pieces, randomly, opening here and there, at odd times, like one would read a book of poems. I remember being struck and awed by Surat al-Zilzal, chapter 99.

During my years at University I was drifting away from Christianity and had stopped going to Church, but my faith in a divine power was deepening. One god, one humanity, one human nature, and human harmony with nature—this was my faith. But it was a little lonely not having a community and a creed.

Independently, I decided to take a year of my university studies abroad. My mother wanted me to go to Paris and learn philosophy. My father wanted me to go to Japan and learn business skill. I wanted to go to Egypt and learn. I didn't know what I wanted to learn, but I knew I wanted to learn it in Egypt. Whatever Egypt had to teach me, I would learn. I was rebelling against family expectations, so I got stubborn and headstrong. I ended up at the American University in Cairo, where I knew nobody and nothing. I studied Arabic with, which I fell in love with. I took a course on Sufism, which had profound effect on me. In Egypt I also entered a mosque for the first time in my life. I wrote a long essay about

Maulana Rumi's mystical poem, "The Masnavi," about the amazing episode where Iblis, the devil, tries to trick Umar ibn al-Khattab into praying at dawn (sound like a paradox? It is. Go read the masnavi!). I prayed *salat* just to see what it felt like, and it felt good. And I met wonderful friends from Palestine, Sudan, Yemen and also from the USA. Nothing dramatic happened, but seeds were planted and insights were gleaned. I came back to the USA to finish my university, determined to study comparative religion and mysticism, and eager to start a PhD that would let me learn Arabic fully. So that's what I did.

Now let's talk about your choosing Islam, or Islam choosing you.

I told you before that my mind moves ahead of my heart. So I decided to do a PhD in Islamic Studies before I ever considered adopting Islam as a religion. I knew that I wanted to learn Arabic and read the Quran myself, as best I could, before accepting what others say about it or a religion based upon it. I also knew that doing a PhD would take me out of the USA for many years, into Islamic spaces and away from my family's expectations. Over the next decade, while doing a PhD at Duke University in North Carolina, I got to live in Pakistan for a year and a half, and in Morocco for two years and a half, and later in India for many years.

It was while living in Morocco and studying Arabic that I really fell in love and lived it out, as best I and he could—considering his family constraints and social obstacles. And it was there, in Morocco, where I first felt that I had already become a Muslim, in my heart first—for once!—long before the idea had occurred to my mind. So I adopted Islam there and then, very simply, during the celebration of the birthday of the patron saint of Morocco, Moulay Idris. I asked my boyfriend to teach me to pray properly, which freaked him out but which he did out of a sense of duty. And I then I walked into a mosque and prayed with everyone in public. No ceremony. No certificate. A little hesitation about finding a new name. A little hardship fasting my first ramazan. But no drama. It felt natural to me and still does.

Queer Jihad

In Morocco, I lived a short walk away from a mosque that was a Sufi center, and I used to go on Thursday nights for *dhikr* meditation, which they do in a beautifully melodious style from Andalusia, and the people there accepted me graciously. Many years later, I found my own Sufi teacher and I am still learning from him. He knows that I am homosexual and it does not seem to matter in his eyes; he has protected me from social pressure to get married but he does not explicitly say that homosexuality is condoned from the viewpoint of shari'ah. He is a Sufi teacher, after all, and not a Mufti. It is his job to train hearts to love fully, not to make pronouncements about the law. So that is how I found Islam—or it found me—and where I am now in the religion.

In an essay that I wrote, I tried to explain to readers who I am as a Muslim, because now that I've written articles and books that some find controversial, that is a pressing concern. Some Muslim critiques question whether I am really a Muslim because of my name and background, so I thought it important to explain this. I'll quote from that essay here:

"I am an American Muslim who grew up in a largely Christian environment but has lived and worked many years in Islamic environments (from Muslim majority contexts like Morocco and Pakistan to Muslim minority contexts like Canada and India). I am a scholar of Islamic religion and culture, with a Ph.D. in Religious Studies, basic training in Islamic disciplines of knowledge (*usul al-din* including the Qur'an, hadith and fiqh), and ability to read and translate Islamic texts in Arabic, Persian and Urdu. I belong to the often-oppressed and silenced minority of homosexuals who, along with transgendered people, exist in all cultures though in different roles. I identify as a gay man who was "out" before I became a Muslim, and am still a gay man after having become a Muslim—some things do not change.... I am a non-sectarian Sunni with a progressive approach to religion. I value the *shari`a* for how its ritual worship offers a means to live an ethically engaged life based upon intellectual principles guided toward humane goals. I approach law (fiqh) as a follower of Abu Hanifa and a reformist within the Hanafi legal method (madhhab) that values rational assessment of traditional sources like hadith reports as essential to the growth and internal renewal *shari`a*. I approach theology (kalam) as an admirer of al-Maturidi, who forged a middle way between extreme rationalists (like the Mu`tazila) and dogmatic literalists (like the Hashawiyya of the past and Hanbalis and Salafis of the present), for al-Maturidi never abandoned dialectic between reason and revelation to achieve human justice, as Sunnis mainly did. I uphold the rational observation of philosophy/science as a student of Ibn Rushd, who affirmed that the natural world is in harmony with revelation and that revelation should be interpreted in ways guided by reason and scientific discovery, not just tradition. I approach ethics (akhlaq) as an adherent to Nizam al-Din Awliya, a Sufi exemplar who taught a delicate balance of love and justice, in which the sincerest way to worship the One who creates all is to care for the many vulnerable with selfless humility."

What inspired you to write your book?

In 2002, I wrote an essay on the topic of homosexuality in Islamic ethics and law. It was meant to be both documentary and critically reformist, written by a Muslim for fellow Muslims. The essay, entitled "Sexuality, Diversity and Ethics in the Agenda of Progressive Muslims" come out in the volume "Progressive Muslims: on Gender, Justice and Pluralism." The editor, Prof. Omid Safi, invited me to write the essay for his book, in which he was gathering the views of Progressive Muslim scholars whose voices could be an antidote to conservative Muslim spokespersons in the wake of the 9/11 attacks.

I was initially hesitant to write about homosexuality and Islam, though I had been investigating the topic for many years; I also felt that including a chapter on homosexuality might undermine the wider project of the book, whose other chapters I also felt strongly about—addressing feminism, gender justice, democracy, inter-religious pluralism, and youth empowerment. My first reaction was to put these other causes first, and say, "Let's address homosexuality and transgender issues later, when democratic commitment and gender justice become stronger in our Muslim community."

Prof. Safi did not accept this reasoning, and that is a tribute to his ethical vision. He challenged me, "Can there be justice and security for some and not for others? Justice is for all or it is for none." He gave me the courage to write. At the same time, I attended my first Al-Fatiha conference in 2002; that was very enlivening to meet so many other LGBTQ Muslims, who were inspiring and also struggling. I saw myself reflected in each of them, in some way, despite their hugely varied backgrounds and incredible diversity. So I resolved to write something for them that might be useful to them in their struggle and might speak of their insights to the wider Muslim community. So many of us gathered at Al-Fatiha conferences (and similar gatherings organized by other

Queer Jihad

support groups around the globe) asking the same questions, pondering the same Qur'anic verses, questioning with the same purported hadith reports, and struggling with the same family issues. Though I wrote the article, I felt it would give voice to the wide network of people active in LGBTQ support groups, and it included many of the insights I had discussed with others in these gatherings, but which were not being written down or published.

As I wrote the article, friends cautioned me and many fellow Muslims were fearful that I might be targeted or even attacked. I knew those concerns came from an urge to protect me, but I tried not to internalize them. I was uncertain about the effect that writing as a Muslim believer and progressive activist would have on my academic career. I was only in my second year as a professor, so would writing as a progressive Muslim on controversial issues damage my prospects for tenure or call into question my "objectivity" as a scholar? Would my Muslim students respect me or would my straight colleagues accept me in this role? Some days I was fearful. Nevertheless, I felt called by my creator to do this, and really felt that it was my destiny to write it, come what may.

The article was published in 2003, and the book as a whole received a lot of attention. Many Muslims found in it a reflection of their own unvoiced concerns, and some started to identify as "Progressive." I did not hear any negative reaction and certainly did not feel any threat—in writing or in person. I think that those who disagreed with my position adopted the strategy of ignoring me in hopes that lack of publicity would bury the issue under silence.

The reactions I did hear were mainly positive and supportive from members of the mainstream Muslim community in North America. Some people, from common believers to Islamic scholars, wrote to me to admit that they had never thought about the issue of diversity of sexuality and gender identity through a theological lens. Several commented that the conceptual tools this essay offered did challenge their assumptions and empowered them to challenge the assumptions of the wider Muslim communities in which they participate on a daily basis. Not surprisingly, I also received many letters from LGBTQ Muslims, who found in the essay a lifeline, as they struggle against family rejection and communal ostracism to find a way to reclaim their religion as their own and voice their own alternative theologies from below and from the margins.

However, some mainstream Muslim scholars also took note of the essay to dismiss its arguments. Interestingly, they have avoided engaging its assertions about the Qur'an and have focused instead on the issue of doctrinal orthodoxy based upon *hadith* reports. These reactions revealed to me the potentially positive intellectual and practical results of a full-scale research project on homosexual and transgender Muslims.

I applied for a two-year research fellowship at ISIM, the Institute for the Study of Islam in the Modern World (at the University of Leiden in the Netherlands). In 2004 I took leave of my teaching position and moved to The Netherlands. At ISIM, I began a project to interview activists, document the activities of support groups, analyze the reactions and denunciations of Neo-Traditionalist Muslims who oppose them, and reflect upon the classical Islamic texts that are relevant to the argument. The book "Homosexuality in Islam" was published in 2010; it includes the theological reflection and textual analysis that I did during those two years in dialogue with many others who participate in LGBTQ support groups around the world.

What should we expect from you in the near future?

The book "Homosexuality in Islam" contains only half of the results of that research project! It is already too long a book for the tastes of many, and I wish that I could have written it in a more concise way. Maybe others will do that better than I can. But I wanted it to be a full engagement with the textual tradition of Islam and also a guide to a critically faithful approach to those texts.

The other half of the project consists of interviews. I wanted the research project to involve real life struggles as well as theological debate. So I invited activists who volunteer in various support groups to give interviews with me about their lives, beliefs,

Queer Jihad

families, loves and activism. The interviews come from support groups on three continents, from activists who live in Muslim minorities in secular democracies. These interviews make up a separate second book, which took a long time to find the light of day. But after many false starts, New York University Press agreed to take up the project, and now the final proofreading is done. The book will come out in November 2013 with the title "Living Out Islam: Voices of Lesbian, Gay and Transgender Muslim Activists."

In every interview that I do, I ask this last question: if you had the power to change something about yourself, what would it be and why?

That is a really hard question, because I don't often think that way about myself and ask "if only…" questions. But I do wish that I were bolder. I'm pretty shy, actually, and there is really no reason to be shy. Life is there only once and, though God is forgiving time is not, so why not take a risk and speak up? I mean this not about activism and politics, but about love and friendship. I don't often speak out openly about how I feel with others, especially those I'm closest too. I trust that they will know how I feel, and I often let opportunities slip by to express myself, to express my love, or gratitude for others. So if I had the power to change this about myself, I would certainly make myself bolder and more outspoken.

To learn more about Scott's book "Homosexuality in Islam," *visit the publisher's website,* <u>oneworld-publications.com</u>

LUDOVIC-MOHAMED ZAHED

The story of of Ludovic is the story of hundreds of thousands of LGBT Muslims worldwide. After realizing he was gay, he felt there was no place for him in Islam and rebelled against his identity as a Muslim. Many young people end up committing suicide because of that conflict, others end up losing themselves anyway by sleepwalking through life, and there are those few whose destructive lives put them in harm's way. The difference between him and many others is that he refused to die away. After a successful life forced him to rethink his spiritual life, Ludovic found his way back to Islam… but only by educating himself more about who he is, his culture, and his faith.

What was your early childhood like?

I was born in Algeria, in Algeirs. I came to Paris when I was two, and so I grew up in Paris. However, my family was going back to Algeria all the time—even if we had just one week of holidays, we would go; every year, sometimes up to four to five times a year. So, I spent a lot of time there.

Did you learn Arabic as a child?

Of course, I was spending my entire summers there. I also studied Islam formally, the Qur'an and the Hadith. Of course, I was studying mostly with *salafi* Muslims.

What was it like being in France most of the time?

Well, I was questioning what it was like being an Arab in France, and being a Muslim in France. You know, there's the racism against you as an Arab; and then, of course, the racism against you as a Muslim. It was a bit challenging. And, then, of course, I'm gay.

When did you first realize you were gay?

Queer Jihad

I have always known that I was different. I knew I was in between; more feminine than boys, but not a girl at the same time. Funnily enough it was actually my father, when I was eight, who pointed it out. He scolded me in front of the family, saying that he would rather kill me and bury me alive than see me like *that*. Of course, he never said what *that* meant, but everybody knew. When I was eleven, when my friends and I were discussing sexuality, I would masculinize myself and I think it was then that I kind of knew what *that* was.

How did you manage it with your other identities?

That's a very good question. When I was twelve, I got myself deeper into Islam. I wanted to know more about the religion, and I dedicated myself for many years. I thought if I had studied Islam more that I would become a "good" person, and that I would be somehow be changed. At this time, I was studying with very conservative guys and in an extremely conservative environment. We didn't talk about sexuality, not at all. When homosexuality came up it was all about the People of Lot, Sodom and Gomorrah, and all of that. So, I spent most of my days studying. At night, when my sexuality would catch up with me I would do whatever I could to repress it.

Being gay was just difficult in the Muslim community, and being Muslim and Arab was very difficult in the French community. I was going back and forth between these communities, both physically and emotionally. I didn't belong to either because there was a rejection from both, but I also belonged to them both at the same time. This was expressed in the relationships I formed with family, friends, and even lovers.

In your book, you discuss a character, Jibril, a young man with whom you fell in love. Let's talk about him.

The man I call Jibril in my book was someone who was nine years older than I was. When I was twelve, I began repressing my sexual identity. This worked for five years. I did everything to repress it. But when I was 17, with Jibril, everything changed. I could not repress it any longer. We were sleeping in the same bed, year after year, and we had intense discussions. We just connected very deeply. It was much more than brotherhood. I was totally in love with him, and I was completely desiring him sexually. So, one night while in bed I talked to him about all of it. He said it would pass, and that I would get married one day and forget all about it. He did end up getting married, but I returned to France to be gay. With Jibril, at that point, I knew for sure I was gay. So, that is what Jibril did for me.

When you returned to France, you rejected Islam. How did you come to that decision?

When I returned to France, I decided to study psychology, to understand myself. I could not continue to be Muslim and gay, it was so hard to be both. I would get up for the prayers and I could not stand; I would get so dizzy because I was feeling completely tortured. I had to decide which one to give up. I decided I could not change being gay but I could reject Islam, and I did. The Islam I knew at that time was very different, because it was telling me that I was a bad person simply for being gay, and I realized for myself that that Islam was not good for me.

You became HIV positive, and this formed a new identity for you. Let's talk about that.

I was infected by my first lover. We were together for a few months, but he was not serious and was not faithful. After becoming positive I realized I was also discriminated, both in the gay community and the mainstream community. Being Arab, gay, HIV positive, everybody was rejecting me for something. So, I decided to live openly with everything and fight.

I started the first organization for young people with HIV in France. It was a social organization, somewhere these young people could go and feel normal. It was somewhere to socialize with others, and to not be a number. Later, I would have the chance to travel to a lot of countries, and be able to meet even more young people with HIV, some even young children.

Queer Jihad

9/11 was a wake up call for a lot of Muslims worldwide. For you, it was the thing that actually brought you back to Islam.

Yes, 9/11 was a big experience for me. I was literally sick for days after the attack, and even went to the doctor. it was such a wake up call for me because I realized these were young people who were killing themselves and others all in the name of religion.

I had been living without spirituality for the ten years prior to the attacks, just working and doing my HIV activism. I talked to my sister, who by the way is also the person I first came out to in my family, about missing something in my life. After the attacks, I went into Buddhism and found a great source of spirituality there.

Buddhism was not as without blame as I had expected. It was also a faith full of cultural conditionings. For example, I found homophobia there. This made me realize that the problems with these religions have to do with culture, which led me to question Islam. It led me to question how the Islam I knew was also influenced by culture.

You were seeing Islam differently, not through the eyes of the naive 17-year-old who felt rejected by family and the man he loved over religion... but through a man who was living in the real world.

Yes, that is exactly it. I was not able to question Islam when I left it. I was following a religion taught to me by others. It wasn't something from me directly, it was my culture. But now I could stand up and actually look at the faith from my own point of view. Amina Wadud says the shit is with the Muslims. I could, for the first time in my life, relate to Islam.

How were you able to do that?

One of the first ways was that I took baby steps. I said to myself there is no way I can pray five times a day, so I did things my own way. But I began to ask the question of "Why should I do this?" every time I was confronted with something in Islam.

Another way was traveling. I went to Muslim countries like Iran and Pakistan, where I encountered Sufism and other types of Islam that I was not familiar with. But then I could relate to some of these things. For example, my family has had a tradition of Sufism. It was interesting to connect to a different view of Islam in different places.

Finally, when I returned to France I was able to look into Islam more academically. I began a PhD program in anthropology and psychology in Islam and sexuality. This allowed me to answer some questions for myself, and understand the faith in a deeper way. It led me to write my book, and to start organizations to reconcile Islam and homosexuality such as CALEM.

Despite having been an activist for many years, you don't like to call yourself one. What do you prefer to call yourself?

I prefer to be an engaged citizen over to being an activist. Activism sounds like someone's job. This is my life. I only want to live my life and spare others from the same pain I went through. This is why I do everything I do.

You do a lot of things, but let's talk about your book. What is it all about, and what does the title mean?

The book is both autobiographical and essays. It talks about my personal life, my background, family, and all that is personal. It doesn't cover everything in my personal life, because, for example, I'm working on another book about my marriage. But the first book also discusses Islam, what I know from the faith, and all of that. The title means "the Qur'an and the Flesh," which is something that is related to France. In France the dominant faith is Christianity, and Christianity has this idea of the flesh of sins. The title was proposed by my publisher because I wanted to call it "Islam and Homosexuality," and they they told me that only gays would buy a book with that title.

How did you meet your husband?

In 2010 I was invited by The Inner Circle in South Africa. While there, I saw a video presentation done by my husband for the organization. I inquired about him because I was attracted to

Queer Jihad

him. Unfortunately, he was not there and I had to wait until the next year to meet him.

What was it like meeting him?

It was amazing. The first time we met, we talked for hours and hours. The next day we began talking about personal things, and slowly we were finding ourselves in a relationship that would mature into a marriage.

Were there ever any cultural clashes between the two of you?

No, not at all. You see, both of us being Muslim and having African backgrounds, there are a lot of similarities. Family in South Africa is just as meddling as that of Algeria. We have similar temperaments as people. No, there haven't been much cultural clashes.

What has been the experience of marrying another Muslim man?

Completely amazing. We got married and our *nikah* was officiated in a mosque. It is such a wonderful experience to be with my husband, I really feel grateful for everything now in my life. This experience has changed my whole outlook on life.

What has been the experience for you as a French citizen marrying a man from South Africa?

Bureaucratically difficult. He came on a tourist visa. He was supposed to go back and apply as he would then qualify under the registered partnership. But we decided it would be too difficult to do that, and now we are paying for it. He's not able to work, even today we went to offices and they always send you around to other offices and it's just a nightmare. But we have hope the marriage laws of next year will make a great deal.

I hope it all works out. What is next for you?

Well, my second book will come out. It's about my marriage, as I said earlier. I will also start an inclusive mosque in Paris. There is a Zen Buddhist temple, which promises to give us space for worship when we are ready. There is also a new progressive organization in the works, it will be a sister organization to Muslim for Progressive Values and other progressive Muslim organizations around the world.

In every interview that I do, I ask this last question: if you had the power to change something about yourself, what would it be and why?

Sometimes I tell my husband, Qiyaam, that I wish I could have had a more simple and peaceful life, not made to fight for human dignity and Allah consciousness. On the other hand, I believe I'm blessed to be part of an inclusive community, progressive Muslims, to contribute to fulfilling the unconditional love of God for all of us. I just wish if anything like reincarnation does exist that this would be my last physical incarnation.

HADIYO JIM'ALE

In the late 1990s, I was introduced to Hadiyo Jim'ale. At the time, she had just finished her graduate studies. She was married, and was raising young children. To top it off, she was in the midst of organizing a conference for the queer Somali community. She had already organized several gatherings in North America, and was headed for her first international gathering in London, where she would bring together over two hundred queer Somalis. I remember thinking what a strong woman is she to be able to do all those things. She really is a woman who can do it all. Little did I know how important she would become in my life, and to the community.

As you know, I love names. What does your name mean?

I'm not really sure. Different people have told me different things about it. I think it means "gift." But there's a word very similar to my name in Arabic and that would mean "alone." I hope that's not it!

Funny. I was wondering because in Somali we say *xadka* when talking about the *hajj* pilgrimage. I wondered if it was related to that. Anyways, let's talk about your childhood in Somalia. What was that like?

It was wonderful. I had a great childhood. We had family in Bosaaso and in Hargeisa. My mother's family is from Bosaaso. Even though we lived in Mogadishu, we went to both places every other year the during the school holidays. I grew up carefree in the streets of Mogadishu, but I would say I equally grew up in all of them. I had milestones in different cities at different ages, and all of these have made great impacts in how I see myself. Therefore I have fond memories of my childhood in these great cities.

That's wonderful. What type of family life did you have?

My parents were both teachers, and that's how they met. We had a very idyllic lifestyle. Modest, for sure. My maternal grandmother raised the kids while the parents worked. We lived not far from the beach and my father would take us there on Fridays after prayer. Financially we were not well off, but my family made it up for having a great love to share. We were very close, and that is what really made the difference for me as a child. It was really nice.

I bet. When did you first realize you were gay?

That's a very difficult question to answer. I grew up in a home of mostly females. My father and brother were the only males out of nine. I was never a tomboy—and I think it didn't help me any—but I never had any objections or ridicule from the other girls. I lived like any other girl. As you know, Somali people don't mix the genders. I spent most of my childhood life with women. I didn't think there was anything wrong when I felt those early attractions. I have witnessed a lot of sensuality between women although not necessarily sexual. Think of it, for example, that it was normal for my grown cousins to trim my pubic hair. I think that sort of sensuality allows a lot of room for someone like myself to flourish. I think I started to wonder when I was a teenager, when I was old enough to know what it meant.

That's very interesting. I have several lesbian friends, and it's amazing how the "lipstick" girls have similar backgrounds to yours. But I would describe you today as butch. Was that something that changed later on?

It started when I was coming out to myself. I think I was probably repressing that part of myself, or perhaps I was using being butch to throw it in front of friends or family who believed it was a passing phase. Before I came out, I lived just like any other woman. I wore the traditional Somali dresses, I painted my hands and nails, I did whatever women did. It just didn't really manifest itself until after I made the decision to accept that I wasn't going to change and that this was my sexuality. I know some men who also had similar experience. A friend of mine, Abdul, who had come out and suddenly he was much more feminine than I had remembered.

You're right; I think it's natural transition for some of us. I remember I once had a boss who used to be so "macho," and then he came out at work and it was like an overnight thing. He became very feminine. How old were you when that happened, when you accepted yourself.

I think I was twenty-four. I had been married for sometime by then, and that really helped me to know for sure that I was a lesbian. Of course, you don't need to marry a man to know you're a lesbian, no of course not. But I mean that it really helped to live with a man year after year, as it really makes it manifest itself in a more natural way. I was sure it wasn't because I was being rebellious, or trying to be unique, it was because this is who I really was. It was more peaceful, too.

Was it difficult, to accept?

Not as difficult as you would imagine. My family is very conservative and very traditional, and they were probably my biggest concern. When I got married, as odd as it may sound to you, I began to feel freer. It was as though marriage provided me with some possibilities. I could be living on my own, of course, with my husband, but it was my house. The more I was with him, the more I began to have peace about it.

I hear that so often. Women who come from the Muslim World often find freedom in marriage, even in marriages they wouldn't have picked for themselves. This is something that people don't talk about. That, really, the family is much more down on the spirit of women.

It was certainly true in my case. I love my family, but they were sucking the life out of me. They were everywhere all the time. It's difficult to find peace and privacy with nine people in the house. You're bound to have someone there at all times. Maybe it was because I knew I was different, but none of my other siblings looked at it the way I did. Some of my sisters were crying when they got married. I was not. I was happy to go. I was ready to go at sixteen!

Queer Jihad

How old were you when you got married, and was it your choice?

I was nineteen. Yeah, I met him at a café. My family was in London at the time, and he was living in Virginia but came to Oxford for a year. I brought him home after six months of sneaking around and dating. My father surprisingly approved, even though he was from a different tribe from us and I had no doubt it was going to be rejected.

I'm assuming at the time you were still hoping to become "normal"?

Oh, yes. I convinced myself that he was going to be the one to help change me. I thought I was horny and that if I got married it would all go away. It's funny how we never stop to think about these things. Thinking back I knew very well I was a lesbian, but I was really in denial. If someone asked me at that stage, I would have said I wasn't with a straight face! Pun intended!

So, you were married to him for five years or so before you came out? Did you come out to him?

No, I told him right away. When I met him, I was very clear about it. I told him that I have this thing going with me and I was sure it would disappear when I got married. He agreed with me, of course! Then we didn't talk about it for two years. After two years he asked one evening if I was still attracted to women. I told him yes, but that it was less. Then I went on and told him I would probably completely change in a few more years. We didn't talk about it again until I asked for a divorce.

I'm sure that was very upsetting for him.

It was very upsetting for me, too! Despite the fact that I wasn't attracted to him anymore at all, he was still the father of my children and had become a very good friend. We had a good life. So, it was upsetting for both of us. He didn't fight me on the divorce and I think that's because he knew I did my best.

You had children together. Do you share custody?

Legally, we don't have any arrangements. The kids lived with me always. After we got divorced, he went to Somali and was there for several years; but when he returned, I went there with the kids. They don't see each other—him and the kids, I mean—but they know they are able to see each other anytime and anywhere. You know, how it's in the Somali community, we don't worry so much about legalities.

That's right. Let's talk about *Queer Somalis*. **I was one of the co-founders, as you, but you really gave it a life back home. Why was that important to you?**

Because I realized that most of the people in Somalia were not going to an online group to discuss the important things that we needed to discuss. Many of them don't have computers and would not feel comfortable doing it in public. Now we have local chapters in Mogadishu, Hargeisa, Bosaaso, and Kismaayo. It's not much but it's small group of people who come together and they help each other.

What are the day-to-day activities like?

Most of the time it's very minimal. Sometimes it's just about going to the local market and having tea with people you know have the same sexuality or will not question your sexuality. Other times we have the opportunity to meet with politicians like the late president of Puntland, who assured us a fairer inclusion in the constitution. Most of the time, it's trying to tell people that Islam does not hate queer people.

How do you achieve that?

By deconstructing their heterocentric history of the faith. Many queer Muslims, for example, are shocked to learn that a gay man lived in the home of the prophet. It blows their minds away because they never stop think something like that is possible. Something else that I tell every young Somali person is that for four years, Muslims in the Islamic Golden Age had an openly gay Caliph or Pope, Caliph al-Amin, the son of Harun al-Rashid. It shocks them in a deep way because they have been taught since a young age that this is not a faith for people like them.

Queer Jihad

I must admit that I too was shocked when I learned about al-Amin from Tabari's "War Between Brothers." How does this type of information help the average queer Muslim?

It empowers them. If you know that type of information then you know Islam is a faith like all faiths, it has room for everyone. There is a certain feeling of being accepted that comes along with knowing something like that. We are seeing less and less traumatized young people because of information like this. They feel more confident and can choose their lives the way that makes sense to them. If a Caliph can be openly gay, surely an average Muslim can also fight for his dignity and rights.

Very well stated. What's next for you?

I'm currently working on my first novel. It's about two Somali women, and how their lives intersect in ways they didn't imagine it would. So, this is the biggest thing I'm working on currently aside from *Queer Somalis*.

In every interview that I do, I ask this last question: if you had the power to change something about yourself, what would it be and why?

This is a very difficult question. I have thought about this over the years, as I watched you ask it other people on *Huriyah*. I think I would change being Somali. I'm not sure if it's as difficult to be anything else. I'm proud to be Somali, but I also know it takes so much energy out of me. It's such a fight, on a daily basis, to continue being Somali.

Interesting that you don't want to change your sexuality, which I suspect is a big part of why you fight so much, but your nationality is something else. This shows how deeply our sexuality is to us.

Yes, of course. I would never want to change my sexuality or the color of my skin or what type of hair I have. These are my deep identities. Nationality, religion, where I live, et cetera, on the other hand, some days I could do without these things.

RUSLAN SHARIPOV

Couple of years ago, we were all shocked to learn about a young journalist and human rights activist who was arrested in Uzbekistan's capital, Tashkent. His name was Ruslan Sharipov. And he was a queer Muslim. Thanks to international media attention, and the continued support from the queer and human rights communities all over the world, Ruslan was finally freed last year. In California, I had the privilege to talk to him about his activism, which led to him being jailed and finally exiled from his homeland. Behind the sweet, soft voice of a small body lies a man whose bravery has taken him to hell and back.

Your name, what is it all about?

I don't know the meaning behind it. It is a common name in the former Soviet Union countries, especially in Russia. In Uzbekistan, it is pronounced as "Rous-tan". You pronounce "T" in place of the "L." But in Russia, and other countries, you pronounce the "L."

Where were you born?

I was born in an ancient city called Bukhara. The Muslims in Uzbekistan call it "Bukhara Shariifa," I don't know what that means, but it is related to the religion.

Did you grow up there?

Yes, I lived there until 1999 when I went to study abroad.

Did you grow up in a Muslim family? I mean, is your family Muslim?

Yes, my family is Muslim. Most of the people in my country are Muslim.

How do you define your sexuality?

I consider myself bisexual now.

Growing up, did you know about your sexuality?

I think it was there, but I don't think I understood. And I didn't have any sexual experience with another man until I came to Atlanta in 1999. When I was in Uzbekistan I already knew about the sexual orientations, but I had more opportunities to see gays and lesbians in Atlanta. I was interested in them. I was interested in everything in America. It just happened that I began to develop a friendship with a man. I didn't know he was of such orientation. The experience happened a few months after I came here.

You went back to Uzbekistan in 2000, what happened?

The government, which sent me to the US on scholarship in the first place, requested that I come back in the summer of 2000. When I did go back, they refused to let me come back to the US. What happened is that I was too active, writing articles that were critical of the government and the system. I was clearly told by the government that Uzbek society was not ready for western-style activism.

Was it true, were you writing back then?

Yes, I was. Mildly, but yes. Coming back from the US, I realized there was a lot of corruption in our system. Everywhere, there was corruption. In the upper and lower levels of the government. So, I was writing about that and other issues.

You wrote some critical stuff later.

After they illegally stopped my studies, I went to different national and international organizations. I complained about the government, about the system. Nothing was helping. So I decided to continue my work with human rights issues. I worked with the Human Rights Society of Uzbekistan and a Russian human rights agency PRIMA. The later, which is based in Moscow, invited me to write for them.

What did the government think of all this?

They did not like it. Writing negatively about the president or other high officers is strictly prohibited. They started to attack me physically on a regular basis. They put me under 24-hour watch. They pressured my family and friends against me. I had no personal life from 2001. They followed me everywhere. I was insulted and physically attacked numerous times in order to intimidate me. It is very dangerous.

Were you thinking about leaving the country?

Oh, yes. I was invited to Russia, United States, and other countries. So they took my passport away. And, of course, they were watching me day and night. That made it impossible for me to leave the country.

The May 26, 2003, arrest. Start from the beginning, what happened?

From 2001, they have warned me. They said that I could be arrested anytime. That I could disappear anytime. That I could be killed anytime. Of course, being in close in touch with international organizations, I didn't think they would do that. They had been trying to find a way to arrest me. The only thing they could do was to bring a criminal case against me based on my non-traditional sexual orientation. As you know, homosexuality in Uzbekistan is illegal and up to three years in jail. I told them that I didn't hide my sexuality.

When you were arrested, where were you sent?

I was arrested in the center of Tashkent, the capital, walking with two of my friends, who were helping me with my work, of course. They took me to the IAD (Internal Affairs Department.) And from there I was transferred to different and different places. The first night they transferred me to another district. And then three days later I was transferred to the IAD's basement. IAD basement was horrible. After ten days, they transferred me to the Tashkent prison.

Were you in the general prison or were you in confinement?

Queer Jihad

Sometimes I was in cells with other people, and sometimes by myself. When I was with other people, I was often with people who were working for the government.

When you were in jail I was reading your papers, and I read that you were beaten and that several times you showed up with bruises in court.

Yes, very much so. I was abused by everybody. The cellmates, the guards and even high-ranking officers. And it was not just beatings. It was gas masks, electric shocks and everything. When I stopped writing, the abuse would stop. Sometimes they found out, other times they didn't. When they did find out, I would get beaten and the electric shock or whatever.

Were you sexually abused?

No, but I was threatened. I was shown video tapes about sexual abuse, and how they force people to tell information by sexually abusing them. And they brought people who they told me were going to sexually abuse me. It was very horrifying.

By the time they arrested you, you had become such an international figure. Were you ever afraid that they were really going to kill you?

No, not after they arrested me. A lot of international media covered my case. It would not have been a good public knowledge if they had killed me.

Is it common for Uzbek human rights activists to get killed in jail?

Yes, of course. A very famous case is Shovruk Ruzimuradov, who was killed in detention in 2001. He was an outspoken critic of the government, a very brave man. He was the leader of the Human Rights Society of Uzbekistan in the Kashkadaria region. So, it does happen frequently.

You were sending letters from prison to various people in the international politics. One letter in particular was sent to UN Secretary Kofi Annan. What came of that letter?

I don't know, really. I was in prison. I didn't send the letter to get a response, and it was a more general letter to the international audience, although directed at the Secretary. It was published in many papers.

In 2004, you had a case review in March. What happened?

I was transferred to house arrest. After much international pressure, they decided they would let me out of jail. But they knew if they gave me complete freedom that I would go back to writing and continue my activism. So they decided on house arrest. I was only able to go to few places. I was still watched by them because they were afraid I was going to get killed by the government's opponents in the system.

They wanted me to stay in jail or leave the country. You see, there are many corrupted groups in the government and they all fight each other. For example, there are two security departments. Unofficially, they carry out horrible activities and blame it on each other. It was in the best of the interest of one of the groups that I stay safe. You see, I was in their custody and if something happened to me they would be blamed. After international scandal, the president might fire the high officials.

I read you went to Russia secretly, how did that happen?

Yes, June of 2004. They could not keep me in house arrest forever. And no one wanted to have me in their system because every group was afraid another opponent group would kill me and they would get blamed. After a while it got really dangerous. One day, they came to me and said if you don't leave today we will not be responsible for your life. So they arranged for me to leave quickly via train.

Were you afraid they would catch you on the way and kill you?

I was very afraid. At the same time, I felt safe that I was still under the protection of the Internal Affairs in Uzbekistan. I still had one more day left under their protection. I knew they would make sure it was safe for me to travel. But I was still scared.

Queer Jihad

What happened when you got to Russia?

While they were trying to figure out what to do with me back in Uzbekistan, I had contacted many embassies. The German embassy, the U.S. embassy, and others. So I had assistance when I arrived in Russia. My documents for political asylum were already in process.

In Russia you learned some pretty scary stuff from the medical community. Let's talk about that.

Yes, when I arrived in Russia I was already very sick. I was rushed to the hospital in ambulance. They diagnosed me with Hepatitis B and D. They said I was very close to dying. They told me it was injected it in my blood. From prison. I stayed in the hospital for a month, and two weeks I was not allowed to walk at all. It was very hard.

They were trying to kill you 'naturally'.

Yes, exactly. Their plan was to get me out of the country and that I would die.

Where was your family all this time?

They were in the USA. They came here when I was in prison because there was an increasing pressure on them.

You joined them October in the US. Did you want to come here or was it because your family was here?

You see, I always wanted to work in Uzbekistan. That is really where I want to be. To this day I'm trying to work in Uzbekistan, even if not physically there. I left my country because my life was in danger. I would never want to be anywhere else.

You once told me that you wished the US would criticize the Uzbek government.

Yes, the US lets the government get away with so much because it is a partner in the war on terror. It is not on any list of caution. And I'm proof that Uzbek government is a terrorist. Yes, I wish the US would criticize that government.

Do you think you will write a book to share your story?

Yes, I'm in the process. There will be a writer who will help me write it.

Well, I for one will be looking forward to that. I think people should read stories like yours so that they understand the world is not all lovely like San Francisco.

Exactly. Here, Americans take everything for granted. Many don't understand how such things can happen out there. We are not all in love.

Very right. Speaking of love, are you in a relationship with anyone right now?

Not here. I don't know anyone here. You see, when I came here my brother told me it is very dangerous to meet people. So I'm scared. It was so easy for me back home. I have a boyfriend in Uzbekistan. We lived together for more than a year, a long term relationship which the government broke up.

Do you think he will ever come here?

I would like to, but I don't know if that is possible.

What would you like to see happen in Muslim countries about queer issues?

It's very complicated. In most of these societies, it is the religion that refuses to recognize the gay and lesbian community. What I really would like to see happen is for governments to stop persecuting people for their sexual orientations. To separate the laws of the countries from the religion. To respect the rights of all citizens.

What are you thoughts on same-sex marriages?

In my opinion, everyone has a right to marry whomever they want to marry.

In every interview that I do, I ask this last question: if you had the power to change something about yourself, what would it be and why?

Queer Jihad

My sexual orientation. It says it is wrong everywhere in the Bible and the Qur'an. I can't change it, but that is what I would change.

IAN IQBAL RASHID

Not everyday do you see a film that deals with being queer and Muslim. In fact, it is very rare. When I first heard of Ian Iqbal Rashid's "Touch of Pink," I didn't know what to expect. I worried it would be another sad exploitation. But that is not at all what the film is about. It is about a young man, like all young men of all faiths, dealing with being queer. I had the opportunity to talk to the man who wrote (from his own life) and directed the film. Here is some of that conversation.

You were born in Africa, raised in North America, and now live in Europe. This is all on top of being queer and having South Asian ethnic background. That is a lot of cultures to juggle. How do you do it?

You know people are who they are. I didn't consciously collect my identities. They evolved organically as my family, and then later I, migrated. I don't juggle these cultures. They co-exist, for the most part, quite comfortably within me. This is just who I happen to be. The problems aren't within me. They tend to come from outside.

Often my own "personal culture" comes up against difficulties: misunderstandings, prejudice, bigotry. I cope with them as best I can—most satisfyingly through my work. But I do have to say that the cities I have chosen for myself, namely London and Toronto, are in many ways the most cosmopolitan, multicultural and multiracial in the world. And though both have their problems, I believe that a greater chance of an understanding of my history and identities exist here in these cities than they do just about anywhere else.

You left Tanzania when you were very young. Do you remember your early childhood there?

Queer Jihad

My family left Tanzania when I was five, but I have quite vivid memories of the place. I remember eating freshly picked mangoes at my grandparents' home, learning to swim in the Indian Ocean, and playing with my cousins in my family's walled garden.

A couple of years back my family returned for the first time for a visit. It had been over thirty years since we left. The first thing we did after arriving was walk to the harbor. It sounds extraordinary, but I could trace my way from the harbor to my grandparents' former home—almost a mile away—completely from memory.

And I have to say I loved being in East Africa. In spite of the pain and difficulties of migration, and my young age when we left, and the strained history between South Asians and Africans in that part of the world, a part of me felt completely at home again in Tanzania. I felt the place sort of claimed me.

What was it like growing up in Canada, being queer and Muslim?

Not easy. On one hand, I had to struggle with a family and community that weren't very understanding about homosexuality, let alone "gay" culture. And on the other hand, South Asians were the newest immigrants and experiencing terrible discrimination in and out of the gay community. Canadians didn't really have an understanding of Muslims or Hindus or Sikhs in those days—we were basically either "East Indian" or "Pakis," depending on who was making the identification. I became involved very early on with an organization called KHUSH, initially a support group for queer South Asian men, which became very important for me. And although the group understandably went through difficulties at times—a pioneering organization trying to fulfill the needs of such a varying and needy bunch of communities and individuals—it was a profoundly important space for me.

You moved to Europe in your early twenties. How did that come about?

I was attracted to the cultural work, particularly the films, being made in the UK and came over to learn from this movement and even be a part of it. People like Isaac Julien, John Akomfrah, Pratibha Parmar, Gurinder Chadha, and Hanif Kureishi were developing a fascinating body of projects and I wanted to be in the place that could generate and foster such exciting cultural work.

Though I have to admit that I didn't expect to stay this long—coming up to 15 years now!—but I met my partner, Peter Ride, and fell in love. He's Australian and was on the verge of moving back to Sydney. I lobbied for Toronto. Neither of us could change the other's mind and so we just stayed put...

I love films and you have captured some beautiful things on film. Did you always want to be a filmmaker?

Thank you, that's very kind of you to say. But no, not at all. I've always loved films and they've played an important part in my development from the time I was a child. But, in a way, fiction has been even more important to me. I've always wanted to write. Before I started working in film, I wrote a couple of volumes of poetry. And I even became a filmmaker through scriptwriting—I worked for many years as a writer for television in the UK. I think I've always wanted to tell stories, in one form or another, that's what has been the driving force.

Which films influenced you the most?

Early Hollywood films. The screwball comedies from the 30's and 40's in particular: the films of Preston Sturges, Ernst Lubitsch, and Howard Hawks. I love the wit and pace of those films. They're like mad journeys through the unconscious of some delightfully dysfunctional peoples' minds.

Your latest film, "Touch of Pink," has generated a worldwide interest. Tell me about how you came to make this film.

I wanted to make an old fashioned Hollywood style romantic comedy like the ones I've always loved. But with someone just like me at the center of it—someone Muslim and queer.

I also wanted to celebrate my family. Their acceptance and, eventually, celebration of my sexuality has been a long and difficult

Queer Jihad

process—for all of us. And it started from such a dark and painful place for me. The film is also a testament to this extraordinary journey that we've all made.

What has been the response from the Muslim community towards the film?

The film—and my life—is set in the Ismaili Muslim community, and it's from here that I've had the most feedback. The response has been mostly positive, and from a huge range of people: gay, straight, young, old, conservative and liberal. But there was a negative campaign generated against the film which began from one Ismaili Muslim woman in Vancouver. She tried to introduce a ban against the film, which I think mostly backfired. The resulting controversy in fact created quite a bit of publicity and interest in the movie.

I've had some hate mail and nasty letters, but the positive ones have hugely outweighed the negative ones. I've tried to write to the nay-sayers, tried to convince them to go to the film and give it a chance. And occasionally I've succeeded, which has been hugely rewarding. You know, it's a very funny and sweet-spirited film. I wanted it to appeal to as broad a range of people as possible without compromising who I am. But in the end, I suppose, you just can't convert everyone.

What is next for you?

I've been very busy promoting the film around the world. I've only just recently been able to start on some new projects—too much in their nascent stages to discuss fully here. One is a British romantic comedy that's very much about food, the other is a Canadian comedy-drama about the long term effects of migration on a Muslim family that came to Canada in the early 70's. I'm also developing a television movie for the BBC—for a season of programs they're developing called "Don't Panic But I'm Islamic."

In every interview that I do, I ask this last question: if you had the power to change something about yourself, what would it be and why?

I wish I was more accepting and tolerant about all the very many things I do want to change about myself. To be kinder to myself. Why? Let me tell you a little story. My little front garden in London contains this weed that I just can't get rid of. I've hacked away at it, tried to poison it, to pave over it and yet it continued to survive and choke my garden. So much energy and time wasted. And so, this year, I gave up and accepted it. I fed and pruned it and watered it and found plants that can co-exist with it. And you know what? Late this summer it gave me the most beautiful little golden flowers. As my wise and loving boyfriend pointed out to me, some people's weeds are other people's wildflowers....

<u>UPDATE:</u> Since this interview was conducted in 2004, Ian Iqbal Rashid had directed "How She Moves," a 2007 feature that follows the life of a young woman whose family tragedy leads to a passion in dance. The film was nominated for a World Cinema Award at the Sundance Film Festival of the same year.

ROB "SALIM" NASH

You probably saw him on VH1, HBO or the many Pride Parades that he rocks with his jokes. Yes, it is Rob Nash (also known to many of us Muslims as simply "Salim"). When I first interacted with Salim, it was through an Internet group for queer Sufis. I remember thinking, "This guy is really funny." Everything he said was funny. Talking on the phone with him, even his language is funny. But beyond his jokes lies a man who deeply cares about social change, who thinks for himself and successfully gets his message across with laugh-out-loud funny performances. Critics everywhere love his "Holy Cross Sucks!," which is a madly funny 30-character saga about three youths going through a Jesuit high school in Texas—all played by him. I interviewed him about his work, life and faith.

I read somewhere that you were born and raised in Houston. What was your childhood like?

Hot, sweaty, humid, mosquito-infested, and surrounded by suburban Republicans. Houston was a fun place, actually. I love my hometown. We suffer from a bit of low self-esteem because we are not Dallas (Thank God!) and we are not Austin (Alas!). The local art and music scene is not supported by the press and the people. Sad, cause we're the 4th largest city and we import most of our Art it seems. We are 1st in smog, though! We took that title years ago from those pussies in LA! Sadly we are only the second fattest city, since those cows in Detroit won fattest city. We'll out-eat those bastards and retake the title, next year, inshallah!

How is Austin?

I lived in Austin when I went to the University of Texas. After 11 years pursuing my dream in LA, NY and SF, I am back. This city is way proud of its music, its theatre, it's comics, its improv, its movies. And all but one of my nephews and nieces lives here, so I get to play my favorite role of all, here "Uncle Wobby."

Tell me about your family. Are you guys close?

We are. I got three brothers and their families here in Austin. My sister, her family and my parents are in Houston. We used to sing in the car as kids on trips to Dallas and lake lbj—how disgustingly Family Von Trap is that? They've been very supportive in my career, in my relationships, and they've been praying and lending shoulders to cry on over my mental illness. Did I mention I'm also the favorite uncle? Gay? Single? Will play with the kids on their terms? I'm a shoe-in.

Growing up Catholic was there any reconciliation between that and being gay?

Yes. But it was a tough fight. 20-30 years ago, the Church was—and sadly to a lesser degree is still—full of homophobic homosexual priests who enforce the homophobia better than the lay people. That's ever changing, alhumdulillah! Many priests are coming out, some leave some remain in the priesthood. And contrary to the headlines, many can keep their hands to themselves. While my Church made lots of mistakes regarding homosexuality, it was also full of very, very loving and heartful people, especially the Jesuits. I went to a Jesuit high school and still have wonderful memories and friends from there.

What was life like as a gay man after you left Catholicism?

Much easier. There was a brief transition when I was sober 5.5 years in AA. So I had the more secular Higher Power of the 12-Step programs. I stopped believing in a Creator, I believed God was an imaginary friend we create to deal with the pain of existence. And He had been co-opted by radical zealots and mind-dead conservatives and liberals. I decided Love was God, but we created Love, it didn't create us. May I confess, my inner Atheist is still alive and well. I still have doubts about God. I hope He doesn't hold that against me.

You are an all-around artist, but you are most known for your jokes. Even talking to you, you are naturally funny. When was the first time you realized you could make a living out of it?

I did an open mike night at the Laff Stop (Now the Capitol City Comedy Club) in Austin in 1987. I overheard other comics saying, "Dude just got back from Waco. Going to Nacogdoches tomorrow." So there was this whole road out there in the late 80s—it's still there, just considerably smaller—and so I set aside my dream of becoming an English teacher and became a standup comic.

You have used comedy to tackles serious issues such as faith and sexuality. Are people more receptive to such discussions through comedy?

I hope so. Or I'm fucked. Laughing at a well-crafted point can bring said point closer to the heart. Debating and arguing about our faith and sexualities, similarities and differences, isn't as fun as laughing at them. Take bigotry; laughing at bigotry is very disarming, especially laughing at our own prejudices takes them out of the underground. When our inner bigots aren't being kept from our honest eyes, and the eyes of those around us, they aren't as powerful.

Your stand-up has been on television, on channels like VH1, HBO and Comedy Central. What are the main differences between live audiences and TV?

TV can really sterilize edgy comedy, which can ruin the edge and dilute the message. It can also soften the edge and make the more conservative element of the audience more receptive to the meat of the joke. TV editing is a bitch too. I've had sets butchered by the editors. Cohesion was lost and I felt it made me look amateurish and unfunny. That's one reason TV and movie actors get reputations for being difficult. It sucks to be misrepresented.

On top of being a comedian, you are also an actor and writer. Which of these talents do you enjoy the most?

I'm supposed to say I love all my children. But that'd be a lie. I like performing my plays more these days than standup, although I'm getting another in a long line of second winds over the past 17 years and enjoying my standup more and more, especially telling Sufi and Muslim jokes. I might be the first out Sufi comic, although these days, I shouldn't claim a moniker I can't prove. Everyone and their camel are doing standup.

You went to a retreat in 2002 and became a sufi there. Was that something you planned on before the retreat?

It was the Jaffe Institute's "Way of the Love." It was the first anniversary of 9-11 too. I knew it was a strong possibility I'd come out quite different than I went in. I'd had two nervous breakdowns from dangerously uncontrollable anxiety. They left me worried I might need to be committed or might hurt myself or someone else through negligence, not violence, inshallah. If I needed to give God another go, I was WAY willing.

You went from being an atheist to being a sufi. That is a huge jump. Were there moments of "What the hell am I doing?"

I still wonder what the hell I'm doing, especially admitting I believe in the *Shaitan*.

Why specifically the Devil?

He's not very fashionable over here as an actual entity. He's way fashionable as a misunderstood icon. He's just a sexy misunderstood heathen, give him a break. Crafty bastard. That sympathy for the devil shit is way seductive, especially as a writer. I love going to hell and exploring the evil side of the *dunya* and beyond. After all, it's my job to tell the truth and delve into all aspects of human experience. I just take God with me when I go, so I don't give in to temptation. I understand the Shaitan to be the darkness, which is more poetic and secular, the disease that's pop psychology or 12-step speak, or the opponent, the Kabbala is way popular here thanks to Madonna. But most Americans think if you believe in Satan, you're disturbed or a Fundamentalist Christian. Not to imply that those terms are mutually exclusive.

How has your life changed since becoming a sufi?

I do many practices. I'm usually successful getting an hour's *zhikr* or remembrance in a day. I copy paragraphs from Sidi Muhammed's "Music of The Soul." I'm not getting to Zhikr much, but I LOVE HALLWA! Which is weird because I was never much into the Rosary or other Catholic things. Praying hours on end in community? Where do I sign up? I'm slowly discovering the voice of God. Discovering my heart. Holding others and myself in the Mercy. I'm also thankful. Like for my apartment, my bed, my covers and pillows and that special time together with friends and my family.

Do you follow a specific Sufi Order?

Shadhuli. I'd like to give a shout out to Sidi Muhammed on the Mount Olives, Word up, Guide! Please pray for us! Blessings, peace, and love to you

You were telling me that you are slowly "coming out" to your comedian friends as a Sufi. How are they taking the news?

If the joke is funny they laugh. I think it's going quite well. My best friend is Greg Walloch. He's a white, disabled comic living in Harlem—cause he likes keeping it real. (His joke.) Anyway, when Greg walks the streets of Harlem, he's pretty safe because he's got crutches, so he's accepted as not too much of a white devil. I'm an able bodied white boy with Texas license plates. In short I'm tha man. So at crack-time, that'd be sundown, when Greg and I leave his apartment, I'm ticking off my prayer beads for protection. We aren't even outside, there's a trans-crack-tion going on in the lobby. I'm not looking anyone in the eye, this is a crack-time rule, doncha know. Greg tells me the pusher was pointing his crucifix at me and my prayer beads as we left the building. Like he didn't want me getting my Sufi ju ju all over his Christian Crack Transaction.

What was your image of Islam prior to becoming a Sufi?

Oh, you know, people stuck in the 5th Century, cutting off hands, killing fags, mutilating vaginas, bombing Jews, kamikazi-ing American buildings. (Not unlike Christians of yore.) My bigoted stereotypes were pretty stereotypical. Mixed in with those images was a knowing that this situation was created and enforced by contemporary Western Colonialism. But I was and still am completely unable to comprehend such suffering; unable to always remember the humility it takes to understand our role in creating and benefiting from this Colonialism and at a loss to know what God wants me to do about this. But I'm listening.

You call yourself "Salim" now. Is there a story behind the choosing of that particular name?

You gotta ask Sidi, he gave me this name. My understanding is he names his Beloveds after a quality or holy person that this Beloved carries. Since anxiety, depression and hyper-vigilance, rage and misery brought me to this path, I know I constructed my *nafs* to cope with the dunya and my broken heart, and my mistaking Shaitan's whispers for good advice. These all veil my true heart, Salim the "Deep Peace."

I know you are single, but what kind of men are you attracted to?

You want the nafs answer or the heart answer? But seriously, folks, I want to hear God's voice in people, particularly men I want to be intimate with. I'm a man; we are suckers for a pretty face. I hope my Beloved will be beautiful on the outside. I think God does want us to be attracted physically to our Beloveds, I want to learn what my heart thinks is beautiful, because often what my nafs think is beautiful is just more of the same dramas I should be sick of by now. This is a challenging part of my walking.

You used to not believe in monogamy. Is that still the case?

I'm still not crazy about it. I know monogamous people who are happy and heart-connected and actually still having sex after several years. If God wants me to be monogamous may he also grant me tons and tons of strength. He hasn't given me any clear guidance on this issue. So, I'm still not a proponent of monogamy for people who want to be poly-amorous.

What are your thoughts on same-sex marriages?

I get so angry and noisy inside over this issue. It gauls and insults me that there's a "debate" over this at all. How dare people debate whether they have a right to withhold marriage from anyone, and fuck their accusing us of "attacking" marriage and family? Excuse me, I must go pray to the *Rahim* now as I want to scream, lecture, curse and break things.

Tell me about the mental illness.

I'm not an early twenty-something embarking on a sexy, exciting career. I'm considered old in my profession. I'm the guy they say, "Something should have happened a long time ago." The "something" I'd been banking since I turned 30 was an off-Broadway opening of "Holy Cross Sucks!" Over the past seven years, the first theatre company let me out of my contract after 3 years of putting off giving me an open night. I had a nervous breakdown right before the firing. After securing a second theatre I had a second nervous breakdown before the final deal was in place. Theatre number two broke our contract when they ran out of money and had to cancel their inaugural season. By that time, I was taking Effexor and Trazadone for anxiety and depression. And I was a few months into my Sufi path. So I moved back to Austin to heal my broken heart.

What were the breakdowns like?

The breakdowns looked like this: can't sleep; can't stop thinking the same anxiety-producing loops of hopelessness and victim hood; paranoia; an inability to control my emotions; despair; passive suicidal thoughts. As I listen to myself tell this story, it is frustrating; I wonder how can I expect anyone to have sympathy for such mental anguish over a silly play. I have no beloved, no house, no kids, all I have is my work. My art is my beloved. And it's fucking brilliant and I couldn't get it in front of an audience to launch a successful solvent career, not built upon poverty and borrowing. It's still very difficult to pay the bills. I'm running out of people to borrow from. I don't know how else to tell it, my heart was devastated.

I know you are doing better now, what helped in that change?

The meds and the path have helped greatly.

What is next for you?

Queer Jihad

I'm currently in talks with Ars Nova, a third theatre in New York who my heart trusts and gets excited about more and more as we work together. We are negotiating a possible opening for "Holy Cross Sucks!" in May. Please pray for us.

In every interview that I do, I ask this last question: if you had the power to change something about yourself, what would it be and why?

I'd be forever young, beecause I miss my younger body. I remember playing tackle football without pads. We'd play kill the man with the ball (Also known as smear the queer) where one guy would get the ball and run until every boy in the neighborhood jumped on top of him. "Smear me!!!" Okay, that was the nafs talking. I would heal my selfishness, my laziness, my cruel streak and the breaks in my heart that still need mending.

<u>UPDATE:</u> Since this interview was conducted in 2004, Rob Nash's "Holy Cross Sucks!" has become an Off-Broadway show! Further, it was chosen as a 2005 top 10 broadway show by *Time Out New York* magazine and the *New York Times* as well as *Variety* gave favorable reviews. Congratulations to Salim! To learn more about Salim and his work, visit his website, robnash.com

YASMENE JABAR

Most of us can't imagine what it is like to be born in the wrong body. Many of us might have experienced the confusion of childhood, when genders are not so easily identifiable, but as we get older things get clearer. For many transsexual persons, life only gets more difficult as the world outside tries to confirm them into what society prefers rather than who they really are. That is why Yasmene Jabar started the "International Transsexual Sisterhood," to help young trans women to understand, accept, and transition. Her story is not just about the life of one woman who overcame a personal struggle but also exemplifies the recent history of the transgender community. Here is some of the conversation I have had with her.

I will start with your name. Tell me the story behind it.

The name "Yasmene" was stuck on me while I was married to my Syrian husband. He gave me the nickname because he said I was his flower, and then all his friends started calling me that. Later, I used it as my professional name when I was a Photographer, and for any other business purpose, but it is not my legal name of which is private and has nothing to do with my professional and public persona.

You were born on a farm in North Carolina. What was your early life like?

I lived a very charmed life for the most part. I knew I was different very early so I spent most of my time to myself on the farm. I learned to love nature and animals, and I spend many hours in the woods pretending to be a Princess or something. I did not trust most people, and especially the boys in school because they were always tormenting me for being different. My family were very close and sort of Mayberryish like in the Andy Griffith Show.

Do you remember the first time you remember feeling "Hey, I'm a girl!"

Queer Jihad

I always felt I was a girl, and when I realized I was not was when my life took a bad turn. I always played dress-up with my cousins, and played with dolls. When I went visiting anybody with my mother, when I was little, I always ended up in the closets dressing up in women's hats and shoes. I loved it. I dressed up so often when I was little that everybody knew about it and most people had photos of me dressed up and thought it was so cute. "Don't he look just like a girl," they would say, "Sssooo pretty." I ate all that talk up and kept wishing I was a girl.

What was it like growing up in a boy's body?

When I became a teenager was when the torment really began. I began to have sexual desires for males, but not as a homosexual male, like a girl is sexually attracted to a boy. I thought more of having my hand held or kissing than actual sex. I never had any kind of sexual relations with any male while I was in school because I did not want the shame that would go with it. But still they called me queer and some even claimed I had oral sex with them when I had not. I never let myself be alone at any time with any of them so it was impossibility. I had all the feelings the other girls had but could not express them. I wanted to be a cheerleader or be a part of their groups and clubs, but of course I could not. I was hormonally intersexed, meaning my body produced more female hormones than male so my body did not change. I never produced facial hair or body hair, my voice did not change and my organs did not fully develop, but my body did grow tall and large, which made me look like a tall big girl. All of this made for a very lonely teenage life with no friends and no social interaction. All I could think of was the time I could leave home and become a real girl.

So you did know you could become a girl when/if you wanted to?

I had learned very early about Christine Jorgenson and also read about others like Canary Cohn, even a girl from North Carolina was in the News for having had a Sex Change so I knew what I was going to do, but just how I was going to get there was still a question that needed lots of answers.

Afdhere Jama

How did you start finding those answers?

Back then without Internet it was hard to find out anything, I remember reading a little ad in the back of a Playboy Magazine about Michael Salem's TV Boutique, so I wrote to them and got a list of books and publications they offered. One was written by Dr. Harry Benjamin about the Transsexual, and the other was a list of pamphlets put out by The Erickson Foundation, which helped Transsexuals. So, I had a very basic understanding of my condition by the time I was fourteen years old.

Did you have any chances to dress up as a teenager?

By the time I got my license to drive a car, I was going out dressed as a girl—just going shopping, to the movies or out to eat. Sometimes I would talk a cousin into going with me, so I would not be alone. At first it was scary, but I got used to it quickly and to the fact that I passed as female better than I did as male. People treated me differently, I was now a real person and my life was beginning to open up for me.

You left home very young. How old were you, and where did you go?

I left home two months after my eighteenth birthday. I had already been going out to Drag Clubs in Charlotte, North Carolina, which was about 25 miles away from the farm where I lived. I will never forget the first time I ever went to a club where Female Impersonators where accepted. It was a valentine's party in 1975 and I was amazed at the beautiful women who were not women. Some turned out later to be Drag Queens, while others were Transsexuals like myself. It was like an awakening for me and I started making friends and plans to move to the big city as soon as I could. I moved to Charlotte a few months later, doing odd jobs at first dressed in what we called plop drag, I was not actually dressed as a girl but wearing unisex clothing and already looking like a girl.

Did people know you were trans?

Most people thought I was a girl. I started taking female hormones at the same time purchased from a black market pharmacy where you'd put down your money on the counter and

Queer Jihad

Jack would give you your monthly bottle of hormones. He later was arrested and went to jail, but he helped many girls who could not have started any other way. I know he helped me. By the time he was arrested I had already had my Sexual Reassignment Surgery.

Tell me about life after you left home?

Soon after I started taking hormones, I began working at a Female Impersonators Club in Charlotte named Orleans. The club was run by an older woman named Olean, who always wore a long blonde wig, and false eyelashes and lots of makeup, who looked more like a drag queen than the real drag queens. I started out just doing shows once in a while then I was hired to be a part of their House Show and worked regular. I became well known during that time, not for my talent but because of my looks. I looked like a real woman and since the crowd was a mix of straight and gay I went over very well to the audience.

You are one of the few transsexual women I know who had the privilege of having a sex change at a such a young age, and at a time when it was neither as popular nor as accepted as today. How old were you, how much did it cost, and how did you come up with the money?

I was making enough money to live, but not enough to save money for my surgery. So, while I was visiting with a Transsexual friend who had worked as a call girl in Charleston, South Carolina, she talked to me about going into that kind of business to make my money. I really had no desire to get mixed up in that lifestyle so I told her I would think about it. I talked to my mother telling her how badly I needed to borrow the money for my surgery, she said I should work and make the money myself. That I would feel I had accomplished something by doing it myself. I told her in what way I thought I could make the money and she said you do what you have to do, and don't worry about what you have to do, just do what you must. After that I went for an interview with Vogue Massage Parlor in Charlotte, and got the Job. But the catch was that the owner did not know I was a Transsexual as she ran a very classy house and all her girls were expected to be top of the line. So I was honored to get hired but at the same time scared to death about it.

Buy that fall I had the money for my breast implants, which I did out patient and was back to work within a week, and within one year I was able to fly to Dr. Stanley Biber for my final surgery. When I come back I went to my parents farm, to get well, and never went back to work as a call girl. I was twenty years old when I had my surgeries. My breast surgery cost $1,000 and my vaginal surgery cost $2,500. But today's prices start at about $10,000 just for vaginal.

In your twenties, you met an Arab man. I know you ended up marrying him, divorcing him, and leaving him behind, but let's talk about how you met and what kind of life you guys shared.

When I met Mo, my first Arab husband, we were both in Collage, he was studying Computer Science, and I was studying Art. We met at a party at the school, a dance I think. He came up to me with the famous line of, "I saw you when you came into the room, and you are the most beautiful woman here." That's all it took. We started dating, fell in love and spent seven up-and-down years together. Our marriage started off very good, we had a good time together as a couple, we went out a lot and he introduce me to a lot of his friends, and family during that time, I thought it would last for ever. He was a handsome ladies man, however. He was a good and loving man, but he had a weakness for other women and that is what caused our marriage to break apart.

When I first found out about his cheating I was in shock and I tried to work things out in my mind for several years before I divorced him. When trust is broken, it's hard to mend it, especially when you are young. But during that time I learned to love Middle Eastern life, I met so many wonderful people, some Muslim and some not, so when we divorced I felt like a big part of my life was over, not just my marriage but my life itself.

Tell me about your current Arab husband. How did you two meet?

I met my current husband Ali, who is from Jordan, on the Internet. We met and became friends over a four-year time frame.

Queer Jihad

At first we were both involved with other people in real life so we were nothing but chat friends, but over time it became more. Finally he sent me a ticket to go visit him in Germany where he had been living for 16 years, during that visit he asked me to marry him. We spent another year apart while I took care of business and he finished his degree. Then we went to Jordan together where we had a traditional Muslim wedding. By the way, he knew about my past from the get go, but his family do not know of my past, and he feels it's not anybody's business as I am completely female in every way.

You became Muslim at a young age, did you convert for your first husband or were you already Muslim?

I did not become Muslim for my husband. I was Muslim when I met him already. I accept Allah as the only God and Muhammad as his Prophet.

You now live in the Arab world, what is that like?

The worst part is having to cover your head on a hot day in Jordan, so I stay inside during the day and only venture out during the evening when it's cooler. The people are great here. So friendly and the families are very close. Of course, the women will ask you very personal questions. I have been asked why I have no children, and will Ali and I have children, so I just say only Allah knows the answer to these questions. Women don't enjoy the freedom that they do in the West, I miss being able to just drive where I want to go when I need to go, but I'm getting used to it. I have a good husband who treats me with love and respect. I would not take a Million Dollars for him; he will be with me for my life long.

What has been your life like since you transitioned?

I feel privileged to be where I am in my life, I had my surgery twenty-eight years ago this year and I thank Allah that I have had such a good life after my surgery. Before my SRS, I had no life at all but now the sky is the limit.

You have set up the International Transsexual Sisterhood, which helps so many tans people around the world, how did you get involved in activism?

I have never considered myself an activist, only that I have a motherly instinct. I wish to help those who need help to find their way. It's like I want to supply a safe home for those who need some comfort. I began with my first support website "Cafe Trans Arabi" because I could find no such support on the Internet for the Trans girls in the Middle East. All I could find was Porno and sex sites but no support to help them find their way with dignity. The other groups simply evolved from that first group to expand and offer support and information and most important fellowship to TS girls around the world.

The Trans Eastern Conference (TEC) is scheduled to take place in Turkey early 2005. Tell me more about this!

TEC is the world's First Transsexual Conference to ever be held in an Islamic country, and it is being produced by TEA Trans Eastern Association. The Conference will have a focus on the hardships of Transsexuals who find themselves in the restricted Muslim World, to help them with answers to their questions and give them support while they make their own choices as what to do with their lives. They should have all the information provided to them, in a safe environment, so they can think clearly as to what is right for them. We hope to have some notable Trans professionals on hand during the Conference such as Dr. Lynn Conway of USA, Christine Burns of UK, Dr. Fatemeh Javaheri of Iran, Adnan Hossain of Bangladesh and Demet Demir of Turkey. For more information your readers can check out the conference's website.

What is next for you?

Who knows? If this event explodes and my cover is blown here in Jordan my husband and myself just might have to relocate to another country, maybe back to the States, but I am sure I will remain active in helping the Transsexuals in what ever way or means that comes to hand.

In every interview that I do, I ask this last question: if you had the power to change something about yourself, what would it be and why?

Queer Jihad

I wish I had finished my education instead of giving it up for marriage. I would feel I had a better foundation to do the things I need to do. But life is a learning tool so we never stop learning.

<u>UPDATE:</u> Since this interview was published in 2004, Jasmene has started a new project called "Transgender Emergency Shelter," which provides immediate shelter to trans persons who are in need of accommodation. To learn more about the "International Transsexual Sisterhood," visit <u>the-sisterhood.net</u>

BADRUDDIN KHAN

The first time I read Badruddin Khan's memoir, "Sex, Longing & Not Belonging: A Gay Muslim's Quest For Love And Meaning," I felt right at home, having understood a lot of what he wrote about and having had experiences not so different from his. Some of these experiences included his undying belief in freedom, and the healthy appetite for traveling, and, of course, sex. In the book, the author is a romantic who finds love in men that are as diverse as can be. His struggles seem to be external ones, as he openly talks about being okay with who he is. It was such a pleasure to interview him.

I have read the book, and liked it very much. What made you want to write about your life?

My life is special, to me. My experiences, and views, may be of some assistance to others that have been through similar circumstances. But, this is not intended to be therapeutic—it is also supposed to be fun to read. I hope readers of all backgrounds can relate to aspects of the book.

What was the hardest subject to talk about?

The hardest subject was the period of my marriage. Marriage is an intimate relationship and I consider myself in general to be an honest person. There is a fundamental dishonesty about getting married to a woman when you are not fully committed emotionally. I felt I had no choice, but that is a reason and an explanation, it does not excuse the act. As a good Muslim, I should have come out much earlier.

In retrospect, do you wish you didn't write about it?

No. Most gay Muslim men face the prospect of socially forced marriage. This is wrong. In fact, I should have talked more about it.

As you know, a lot of gay Muslims get married to women. What would you say to someone who is planning to do that?

Queer Jihad

Don't get married to a woman unless you are prepared to be there for her, physically, emotionally, and sexually. It is not right, it is dishonest, and it is Un-Islamic. As a good Muslim, it is incumbent on you to enjoy the gift of sexuality. If you want a man, and if you find a consenting man, have him. If you want a serious relationship, and are prepared to make a mutual commitment with another man, by all means, do it! If you are forced by circumstances to marry a woman, be kind to her, giver her kids, treat her well, and find yourself a male lover who can be friend to her. If you don't find a lover who she accepts, you will become promiscuous and distant. If you abstain from the natural pleasure of sex, you will express your anger in indirect ways. In the long term, sexual desire will not be denied, in one way or another.

What are your views on gay marriages?

Necessary. How else can two men make an enduring public commitment?

In the book, at the end, one gets the sense that you were giving up on Pakistan, that you felt like it wasn't your home anymore. Is that the case?

I have not given up on Pakistan. Pakistan is always part of me. But it is only a part of me and not all of me. It is my history, but not my foundation today. One grows up and puts history in context.

Your close friend from the book, Aurangzeb, who also happens to be gay, and you have chosen completely different lives. When that happens, generally, friendships slowly fade out. Is your friendship still there?

Yes, it is. Our lives are different, but when we come together we connect back to old times. He has family and frequent sex on demand. I have the love of a man and occasional sex, and I clean my own house! Sometimes, I would rather have naked boys with brooms running around the house, but in general I am satisfied.

What can we expect from you in the near future?

Another book, sometime soon! I am working on it, but progress is slow. I have too many demands on my time.

Do you have anything you would like to say to your readers?

Yes, just that life is a gift. It is meant to be enjoyed responsibly. Make yourself happy, make others happy, and you are doing God's work. Build great things and do whatever good you are capable of. Live without fear of any mortal man and live with passion for all.

In every interview that I do, I ask this last question: if you had the power to change something about yourself, what would it be and why?

Nothing, really. I am quite happy and content. I strive every day to do my best, and that is good enough. But, yes, if I could make love the way I did at 20…Ah, yes, I would change that about me!

<u>UPDATE:</u> This interview was originally published in the 2002, I have been in touch with Badruddin since and he's living a quiet life. He recently told me he's working on a second edition of his first book, as well as a new book.

WAEL K.

Between living in the Middle East where he was born, Europe where he kind of grew up, and America where he currently lives, singer/songwriter Wael K. was influenced by diverse music. But Wael has created his own genre of music. His album, "Identity Crisis: Aliens, Beduins and Leos," was just released. Reflection of the diverse musical influences in his life, this album is full of really cool songs. So cool, actually, that most songs are being played on radios all over the world. Being the product of a collaboration of more than fifty people, this album is so good. I met the musician at a party in San Francisco where we danced to his tracks. He is a very cool, down to earth kind of guy. We talked about our common interests in music. Later, I was honored when he agreed to let me interview him.

Let's start with your name. What does it mean?

For the longest time, I was under the impression that "Wael" was one of those rare Arabic names that have no meaning, but about two years ago I had dinner at a cousin's relative's home. This man's a linguistic scholar who's very knowledgeable when it comes to old Arabic names, so when my cousin asked him what my name meant the guy told us that "it refers to someone who leaves the place he's from, goes somewhere else, and survives." Basically, according to this wise man, "Wael" means "Survivor."

You have roots both in Syria and Saudi Arabia.

Yes, I was born in Damascus, Syria, but grew up in Jeddah, Saudi Arabia, because my parents lived there. They still do. My father was born in Mecca, Saudi Arabia, my mother, like me, was born in Damascus, and my brother was born in Vienna, Austria.

What was your childhood like?

For the most part, my childhood was a good one. I remember I wasn't always very social and spent a lot of time listening to music, creating dream or imaginary worlds, and playing by myself. Don't get me wrong, I had a lot of friends I played with, but I definitely appreciated and valued time alone. In fact, I still do.

How was music perceived in your family?

My parents, brother, and I listened to all kinds of music. In our home, you could hear everything from Arabic music by Fairuz & Umm Kalthoum to African Music from Kenya and South Africa, and from French, Spanish, and Italian artists to Stevie Wonder & The Rolling Stones, Disco to Rock & Roll, Metal to Pop. You name it, and we probably listened to it.

Were you interested in music more than the rest of the family?

We all loved music, but growing up, I was definitely the music addict in the family. It seemed like I always had my tapes and ghetto blaster or Walkman with me everywhere I went. I guess they were like my security blanket. I used to make a lot of mixed tapes of my favorite songs. To this day, when I get into my parents' car they're always expecting me to hand them a tape. I trained my parents well. So, my parents love music but never thought it could be a serious career choice for one of their sons. None of us dreamed that one day I would be handing them a CD of my own songs.

How did the opportunity to go to Switzerland for boarding school come up?

I went to a public school in Jeddah, where I did my studies in Arabic, until I was about 11 years old. I was then given the option of staying in the public school in Saudi or going to a boarding school in a small village in Switzerland. I jumped at the opportunity of being able to pursue my studies in English at the boarding school, because my English was better than my public school English teacher's at the time, and I think I felt I needed more of a challenge. Also, I was beginning to feel like I needed a little more independence from my parents and I had a lot I needed to work out by myself. Besides, my brother and three of our childhood friends (who are all older than me) were waiting for me to join them.

My father worked his ass off so he could afford to send my brother and I to Switzerland, and I will always be grateful to him for that. My mom also sacrificed a lot personally to let me go to Switzerland, and I love her for that.

What was your experience there like?

I never really liked or cared about schools as institutions, per se, because I still believe self-education and the interactions and experiences you have with friends and fellow students teach you a lot more than the classroom ever could. That said, boarding school was an incredible experience, because I made friends for life. My friends in boarding school became my family. It wasn't always easy, but I learned a lot about life, myself, and other people.

What did you study?

For a long time, I didn't really know what I wanted to do with my life, but I knew I loved words & different languages, so I got away with being the only student I know who took four languages and no other subjects his last year of high school. Because the school in Switzerland was very international and had students from all over the world, it was easy to pick up new words and practice with friends.

You started writing music as a teenager. Tell me about that.

For a couple of summers, when I was in my late teens I had enjoyed working at a Safeway Supermarket in Jeddah, but I didn't apply for a job there the summer I graduated from boarding school, because I was getting ready for college and my parents were taking my brother and I to the South of France.

Anyway, because I didn't have a summer job, that summer felt pretty long at times, even in the South of France, so one day I began writing in a notebook. I wrote anything that popped into my head, in other words, feelings, thoughts, emotions, and ideas. A few days later, I looked over what I had written and realized that 95% of it rhymed, even though I wasn't trying to write poetry or songs. Pages and pages of mostly personal stuff came out rhyming, and I figured it was because I loved and listened to so much music as a kid. So, I didn't actually write music, but I filled notebooks, napkins, scraps of paper, and anything else I could get my hands on with words that some consider musical. I discovered writing by accident, and find it very therapeutic.

For many years, I hid what I was writing, even from my closest friends. A few of my friends would ask me what I was writing in my notebooks, but I would tell them it was nothing, because I felt it was very personal. It wasn't until I realized I might have to make a living sharing my words and ideas with people that I allowed close friends to read some of my stuff.

Your CD is by "The Iambic Dream Project." What does that mean? Is that the name of a band?

I got the name from "The Iambic Pentameter" which is a poetic term. I was looking for something that could allude to a poetic dream that began with words that rhymed, and something that abbreviated into I.D., because the songs contain parts of my identity. I didn't want to use my name for the CD, because I wanted to show that, although it was originally my dream and vision, many people contributed their talents and skills to help make it happen. "The Iambic Dream Project" is a poetic dream I've subconsciously always had of creating a CD with an eclectic mix of songs, but thirty eight amazing singers and musicians, fourteen incredible recording and mixing engineers, an unbelievable mastering engineer, two gifted photographers, a great graphic designer, many loving friends and family members, and a brilliant producer/voice coach/vocalist/songwriting partner and friend named Raz Kennedy made it possible.

Raz Kennedy co-wrote the music and also co-produced the album. How did you two meet and how did your collaboration begin?

I met Raz through my friend Shana Morrison, who's a great singer. I think Shana had worked with Raz once or twice, and she recommended him to me when I asked her about a good voice coach. I didn't really want to sing, but fell into it, because in the past I had worked with a couple of very talented singers who loved my lyrics and asked if they could sing my songs, but their interpretation of my words didn't feel right to me. Their vocal technique was there, but they were missing something essential in my stories: the emotions behind them. Anyway, I wanted to develop my words and melodies into more complete songs, and I figured if I could sing my words I could finish writing them.

Initially, I began working on and singing other people's songs, but when I mentioned to Raz that I wrote my own lyrics he asked me to bring some of them in. When Raz read some of my words he really liked them, and his faith in my lyrics triggered me to suggest he help me with the music. We began collaborating after that. I would bring mostly finished lyrics and some raw melodies I had sung acappella into a tape recorder. He would listen to the tape a couple of times then he would play the chords from the rough melodies he heard, before we would develop them further.

Raz has a great ear and a wonderful musical imagination. He was very instrumental, pun intended, in helping me finish my songs. Musically, our collaboration was very organic. We would finish a song in about thirty minutes or so. He created a very safe space for me where I felt I could share some very intimate stories through my lyrics. After about ten or twelve weeks of meeting once or twice a week, we had about thirteen songs that we really liked, so I suggested we record them and asked him to help me produce an album. He's really the main producer, especially when it comes to the music and vocal arrangements. That's how The Iambic Dream Project's CD began.

In the album liner notes you dedicate it to your 'kids' who have similar names. Tell me more about that.

I dedicated the album to my niece Basma, and my kids Alien, Beduin, and Leona. Alien was our family German Shepherd, and Beduin was my cat. Both of them passed away some years ago. My cat Leona is still with me.

My brother and I adopted Alien when we were living in L.A., the cats and I adopted each other (at different times) also in L.A. I didn't name any of them, but, to me, their names are symbolic of

Queer Jihad

how we are sometimes born strange and different like aliens, grow up wandering the desert we call life like nomads or beduins, and hopefully overcome struggles, we encounter along the way, with the strength of lions or Leos.

Most of the songs from the album are now being played on the radio. Even famous singers don't get the chance to have most of their songs from a particular album being on the radio. How does it feel?

It's amazing! It feels like a dream. I'm thrilled, but I had never really thought that far ahead. Most of the time, I was so involved in trying to create something with Raz that we would both be proud of that it didn't occur to me that someday some radio stations would play eight of our songs.

When did you come out to yourself?

I'd always known I was different. Actually, there are so many of us that "different" sounds like an oxymoron. Anyway, I'd known for a long time, but was in denial and didn't really come out to myself completely until I was in my early twenties.

Does your family know?

Yes, I came out to them when I was twenty-three, because I wanted to bridge a gap I had created between us by not being honest (with them) about a big part of who I am.

Do they listen to the CD?

Yes, my family continues to listen to it. They really like it and are very proud of my work, and that makes me extremely happy. Without my parents and brother, I wouldn't have been able to end up with this professionally recorded album. I've never really had the financial means to support my dreams fully, and my family has always been generous in the way they've invested in my dreams. I'll always be grateful to them, and I'm hoping to make enough money to help put my nieces through school.

As you know, I went to the party where people had the chance to listen to your album and I asked a few people what they thought. Some of them really thought this was the work

of a genius and all of them enjoyed the music. What has been the response the album gets from the general public?

Genius? Madman, maybe, but not genius. People are too kind. Either way, as I've mentioned before, I can't take all the credit. Most people really seem to like the album, but some people don't really get it, because it's so eclectic. I think the majority of people like most of the songs, but you can't please everyone. As much as I like hearing that people like the album, it's really more about challenging myself as a songwriter and singer, and sharing a variety of genres I enjoy working in.

I really love all the songs from this album, particularly "The Boys of the BLVD.," which I think is one of the most beautiful songs I have ever heard, both lyrically and music-wise. What is the story behind it?

Thank you very much! I'm thrilled that you like my music. "The Boys of the Blvd." was the first song I finished lyrically. Most of the words were written when I was in my late teens. I think I was nineteen at the time, and I was in Switzerland for The Montreux Jazz Festival. People always ask me about that song and if it was inspired by real life gay male prostitutes whom I noticed on the streets or something like that, but the truth is I was at a park in Montreux one Sunday afternoon. It was a beautiful sunny day, there were no prostitutes around, and I was feeling good when the words to that song suddenly popped into my head, so I wrote them down on paper.

My songs always come out multi-layered somehow, when it comes to the storylines. I think it's because I try to allow the words to come out of me without judging or critiquing them. So, "The Boys of the Blvd." is about more than prostitution. It tackles subconscious fears I had growing up of possibly being kicked out of my parents' home if they knew I was gay, even if I never acted on my sexuality.

There's also this very subtle love story between two of the boys, but it's so subtle only I know about it. It's really more about them helping and supporting each other, running from the cops

Queer Jihad

and bad johns together, etc. It's a part of the story that I've always envisioned would be unveiled in a music video for the song.

Are you in a relationship?

No. My friends are gonna love this question, because a few of them claim my long term self-imposed celibacy is more severe than that of a monk (living) in a monastery. I'm open to having a relationship, but I'm extremely picky. He'd have to be extremely special, because I don't put up with much crap, and he would have to be strong enough to call me on any of my own crap. In the mean time, I'm enjoying the relationship I've been having with my music for the past three years. I wanna keep nurturing that.

What are your thoughts on same-sex marriages?

I think the legal rights and benefits that come with marriage should be afforded to all human beings who choose to be in loving, monogamous relationships, regardless of their partners' genders. On the other hand, I don't need a piece of paper to tell me that my partner and I love and cherish one another. I would only get "married" if my partner really wanted to. Many straight people take marriage for granted. I mean look at the rate of infidelity and divorce, and some of them have the balls to tell us we're not worthy of a real "marriage."

What is next for you?

I'll continue to get the word out about my songs, and hopefully make enough money by selling my CDs and getting songs placed in film and television, and sung by other artists, so that I can afford to record and put out the next Iambic Dream Project album. I have so many stories waiting to be told.

In every interview that I do, I ask this last question: if you had the power to change something about yourself, what would it be and why?

There are many things I'm working on changing. I believe I'm a work in progress, and I want to keep evolving. But if I had to pick two things - sorry I can't narrow it down to one - they would be to be less of a perfectionist and to be more patient with myself and others. I would change those two things, because both interfere with my humanity, creativity, and relationships with people I love.

For more information about the album, including listening to the first two minutes of all the songs, and buying a copy of the CD, visit the official website at iambicdream.com

FARZANA DOCTOR

Farzana Doctor is a long-time activist with "Salaam ," the LGBT Muslim organization, and a therapist who works with the community. As such she remains an important member of the local queer Muslim community, as well as the local Bhora community, of Toronto. She is the author of "Stealing Nasreen," an irresistible novel that features an Indo-Canadian Muslim lesbian who gets entangled in the lives of an Indian couple who recently immigrated to Canada.

Where were you born?

I was born in Zambia.

Tell me about your African background.

Well, my parents are originally from Bombay. They spent five years in Zambia, and that is where my sister and I were born. We spent short time there, so mostly I say we are from India because that is sort of where all the family is.

How long were you yourself in Zambia, and do you remember it?

No, I was only in Zambia until I was six months old. So, I don't really have any history there.

When did your family come to Canada?

We came to Canada in 1971. I was, of course, only six months old. We came directly from Zambia.

So, you never lived in India?

No, I have never lived there. I visited a lot. I have spent most of my life in Canada.

A lot of immigrants feel a pressure to assimilate into their new countries. Have you had similar experiences in Canada?

I grew up in an small town in Ontario. And there was pressure to assimilate, but I don't think we did. There is a small community of Indians here and we were quite involved in it. So, I had a lot of South Asians around... socially growing up. Of course, all my neighbors were white. All my classmates were white. But we knew we were Indian—and there was an emphasis on Indian culture—while being part of an area of mostly white.

Did you have a hard time reconciling the cultures as a child?

When you grow up in a town with a large majority of whites, I think it does cause complications for identity development because it is such a racist environment. Everything gets distorted, including your sense of beauty.

Toronto is such a diverse city, when did you move there?

Yes, it is such a wonderful city to live in because it is so diverse. There is a thriving queer South Asian, queer Muslim, and queer of color community. So, that is really great! The small town I had lived in is only an hour away from Toronto, but I had moved to Toronto in 1993 and have been living here ever since.

Did you always want to be a writer?

No. I always wrote, but my writing slowed down a bit once I reached university. I think part of it is just writing essays and all that makes you not interested in writing creatively, but I did continue to write here and there, and wrote poetry as well.

Yes, I had seen your poetry before. When did you get interested in writing again?

About eight years ago or so, I started to make an effort to sit down and write. And that came following a writing class through the School of Continuing Studies here at the University of Toronto. It was a course called "Writing the Novel." Since that class I had started a writing practice. In the last few years, I made a lot of effort to be a writer. For example, I quit a demanding job just so that I could work part time and also write.

How did "Stealing Nasreen" come about?

Afdhere Jama

At the writing class, I wrote what was the first draft of what is now the first chapter of the book. After writing that first draft, I felt there was more to the story. I didn't quite know at first that it would be a novel, but I knew it was a story that would go somewhere. I thought it would be a short story, but it kept growing.

The book is based on a professional Indo-Canadian lesbian who kinda falls in love with the lives of two immigrant Indians. Is that an accurate picture?

I don't know that I would describe the last part that way. I would say she has got a number of struggles and gets sort of enmeshed in the lives of Salma and Shaffiq by accident. That brings a struggle for her but it brings a particular struggle for them. But she is struggling with dealing her own break-up, and her difficult relationship with her father.

What do people see as the main story?

You know, everyone has been telling me something different. I actually see the main story being more about Shaffiq and Salma.

I see the main story as being more about Shaffiq.

I started writing Shaffiq, he was the first character. And the story sort of evolved from there.

What inspired you to write his story?

At the time I was writing his story, there was a lot of discussion in Toronto—and there still is, but it started to be some discussion back the—about the severe underemployment of a lot of professional immigrants. So many people were not getting work in their field. There was an urban myth, which I think was partly true, that every taxi driver in Toronto is a surgeon from another country. I always knew about this issue, but the discussions made me a little bit sensitive to it. So, that is where Shaffiq came from.

What an interesting background. And what about Nasreen, I kinda think it was inspired by your own life. Am I wrong?

Queer Jihad

Not entirely. I was new to writing at the time and I thought it would be helpful to me to choose a frame that was not too far from my own life. And that was the frame of an Indo-Canadian lesbian who works in a hospital. That is really where my similarities end with Nasreen, and, of course, the rest of her are fictionalized pieces of other lives. There are things happening in her life that are from my life—

Like the therapy scenes?

Yes, I could write those therapy scenes because I'm familiar with that as a therapist, but I'm not the same kind of therapist. She is more mainstream, and is far more burnt out. But also like the break-up scene at the bar—that stuff has happened to people I know.

Obviously you have different fathers.

Yes, different fathers; different social lives; different hangouts—we are just really different in those terms.

Salma is very interesting also, is she based on anyone in particular?

She is a character that I made up. Some of the issues she is dealing with are issues that I have heard about from people in terms of their experiences in living in India. She is not really based on anyone in particular, but grew from a very imaginative place.

Did you plan the relationship dynamics in the book?

No, it was pretty organic. I would say it wasn't until maybe through a third of the book that I really started to play with it. But the characters and the story developed. I have often wondered what is the best way to write.

How do you work as a writer, do you know where you are going with the story ahead of time?

I always write organically, but a part of me is always thinking, "I wish I knew where I am going!"

The book has such a great story. Was it difficult finding a publisher?

Afdhere Jama

Yes! It took me two years. It was a long and discouraging process. You know how that works—you get a lot of rejection. I finally found this small feminist press, based out of York University. It is very small—a one-woman operation. She has this real dedication to try to publish work that might not be otherwise published. So, I'm very grateful that she published it. I'm working very hard doing a lot of self promotion as a way to get it out there.

Were there any concerns for safety, did you ever want to write under a pen name?

I did have mild fears about being out there as a queer Muslim person. Through my work with "Salaam," I got a death threat. That was quiet scary. It was over e-mail but it is still scary to receive it. I did have some thoughts of, "Ok, this book is about a lesbian and there are Muslims in it—what would that exposure bring me?" So, I do have a little nervousness about that, but not enough to want to write under a different name.

Are you active in the queer Muslim community in Toronto?

Yes. For a few years, I was very involved. I was coordinator for "Salaam"—I think there are something like ten coordinators for the organization in Toronto, and I was one of them. And in the last six months, I kind of stepped aside because I needed to have more time for the book. But I'm still involved, and I still see people around. So, I'm still a member of "Salaam."

What about your relationship with Islam—how is that?

Hhhmm. That is an interesting question. I guess that is important here because you are a Muslim publication, so that makes sense. I call myself these days—and it has changed over the years—but I consider myself a secular Muslim.

What does being a secular Muslim mean to you?

For me, it means that my connection with Islam is more cultural and political versus religious. I didn't grow up in a religious household, so that is part of why I feel that way. But also I consider myself a spiritual person and the kind of Islam I have been exposed to has been more accepting than some other forms of Islam that other queer Muslims might follow. I'm a Bhora.

That is part of Shi'a, right?

Yes, I'm from a Bhora background.

Are you out in the Bhora community?

Very much so. They are just open minded, and are very accepting towards me. At least no one says anything bad in my face, I don't care what people think on their own. I very much value the Bhora community. I very much value Islam. But not in practicing.

I heard they are mostly concentrated in India. Are there going to be any translations of the book in India?

Yes, the publisher is actually working on that. She is submitting to different publishers in India. I also asked her to look into UK publishers who might want to publish a European version. She is also trying to see if there will be a film edition. So, she is investigating all that and we will see what happens.

Yes, it would make a very good Mira Nair film!

Well, we sent it to her so lets hope. That would be quiet a dream, right?

What is coming up for you after this book?

I'm working on a second novel. I started working on it couple of years ago while I was still waiting for a publisher. I'm about a third of the way through of the first draft. I haven't been doing much writing in the past six months, because I had been entangled in the publishing and promotion of this book, but my goal is to complete the second novel by spring of next year.

Oh, good! We will be looking forward to that. In every interview that I do, I ask this last question: if you had the power to change something about yourself, what would it be and why?

Afdhere Jama

Hhmm. I don't think I would change anything about myself. I know there are things I would want to change in the world!

<u>UPDATE:</u> Since this interview was conducted in 2008, Farzana had a second novel published. The novel, entitled "Six Metres of Pavement" and published in 2011, was a 2012 Lambda Literary Award winner for lesbian fiction.

RAHAL EKS

Rahal Eks has lived it all. No, really, he has. He has lived all over the world, interacted with many different cultures in a personal way, and found himself in different experiences to make a wholesome identity so strong not even he can break it. From mescalin trips in the mountains of Peru to finding Sufism in Spain, from educating years in the United States to love life in Morocco, Rahal has found that home is wherever the heart is. What stands out about him most is his intense unique nature. There really isn't anyone like him.

I will start with your name, "Rahal," which means "nomad" in Arabic, what does it mean for you?

There is a Latin saying, "nomen est omen," and indeed my name is a rather perfect description of my nomadic background as a given fact and also of my chosen lifestyle. I would add, "once a nomad, always a nomad"—it's like being queer, you remain that way, no matter what. "Ana rahal," I'm nomadic in more than one way.

Where were you born?

I was born in Alexandria, Egypt, to an unmarried young Muslim girl. My father was Italian, and a passing phenomenon I never met.

What was your childhood like?

My childhood was very un-Egyptian because I was adopted as a baby by a German couple and spent my childhood in what I considered a most alien country. Not that my adoptive parents were horrible, au contraire, but I felt just out of place and I wasn't any good at fitting in with my fiery Leo-Arab-Latino temperament.

You tried to leave from that environment several times. Let's talk about that.

The first time I ran away from "home" I was five years old. One day, when my adoptive parents had annoyed me with their

Queer Jihad

German ways, I decided to take off and go south, because that's where I knew my place of belonging was located. I packed my favorite toys, a Teddy Bear included, some clothes and walked across town. I got as far as my grandmother's apartment, where I had planned my first stop over. She took me in, but of course she returned me the next day. In other words my first flight was of short duration, but I'm proud that I tried it.

The second incident was a couple of years later, when going for a walk with my adoptive parents through a forest. There was a gypsy camp. When I heard that gypsies travel the world I was going join them and take off, my adoptive folks literally had to hold me back. Evidently under loud protests on my part, and swearing that I'd take off to discover the world as soon as I'll have a chance... and I did! *Al-hamdulillah!*

You sound like you were persistent. How old were you when you finally left, and where did you go?

Si señor, I certainly was. At 19 I left and migrated to Spain, that's when my free self-determined life began.

When did you first realize you were queer?

It was at the beginning of puberty, I fell in love with a Spanish migrant boy called Pepito, who looked rather Moorish. The Germans called him a "Gastarbeiterkind," the child of a guest worker. I thought this weird word construction was rather perverse. I have no idea what other kids called me behind my back, but in those days racism and xenophobia were kind of low key.

What happened with Pepito?

Nothing really happened with Pepito, I just watched him play football, even though I hated sports, and occasionally I talked to him. From him, and his younger brother, I picked up my first Spanish words: *"Cállate la boca, cabrón!"* (Shut up, you goat!). But I wouldn't say I knew at that young age what queer really meant. I just fell in love with Pepito and felt this sexual attraction for another male, thinking it was perfectly normal—and, of course, it is—but later I found out that society had different ideas on homosexuality.

Afdhere Jama

When was the first time you met other queers?

It was perhaps a year later, I was 12, when I went with my school choir for an extended stay to Paris. There I ran into a bunch of North Africans who were openly gay and who took a liking to me. I was thrilled. What held me back were some snotty and quite homophobic comments by some of my buddies from the choir... So I went out with a French-Jewish girl to prove being as straight as an arrow, while at night I secretly jerked off over fantasies with the North Africans.

How long did your "straight" life last?

Until the age of 17 I pretended to be straight. Then this openly gay guy kissed me on the lips, and I knew I was getting ready to really have sex with a man. Soon I did. Shortly after, I fell in love with a beautiful half-Persian boy, followed by an affair with a hot Moroccan...

Where were you having all these hot affairs at 17?

I was in Hamburg at that time, eager to take off.

You have lived in some countries where the largest population is Muslim, such as the UAE, Egypt, Morocco, etc. Was it more difficult being queer in those countries?

Actually I had the time of my life in the UAE and in Morocco. Egypt was fun too, but somewhat more conservative. I was there way before the Queen Boat affair when things were still quite cute and dandy. I had the luck to live in those countries before the rise of current increased fundamentalism. It was still a different time, more tolerant and diverse. In other words, I still experienced a kind of "golden epoch."

I also have to point out that my position was somewhat special: I never had any family breathing down my neck. I was on my own, which is a big plus point in terms of privacy and personal freedom. And I was Arab enough to be considered one of them, yet having a passport from Europe always gave me the option to take off without having to apply for a visa in case the shit hit the fan. During that period, I definitely felt happier and totally safe in the

Queer Jihad

Arab world than in the West. I wouldn't say this now. Times have changed and in many ways things have gone retrograde.

What do you think is the main cause of this change in the Arab World?

Islamic fundamentalism is the main reason for this change of atmosphere. During my last stay in Marrakesh I was quite horrified how things have changed for the worse.

It sounds like you had the best of both worlds, having Eastern and Western parts of you. It also gives you a better viewpoint, I think, than those who are one or the other—always seeing things from just one point of view. Obviously, change is inevitable. In what ways, do you think, the West has changed?

Yeah, that's right, I somehow feel like a walking satellite TV station, with many channels I can freely choose from at any time: there is my European program and a North American one—I lived also five years in the United States, and that left some traces too—my Latin American soaps, and my Arab series, not to forget the Spanish channel, and feeling very much at home with Iranian, Afghan, and Indian/Pakistani cultures due to my involvement with different Sufi teachers.

Funnily enough my Occidental side is more American than anything else, and my Arab side is very colored from my time with the Bedouins in the UAE. I can also have two or three programs running at the same time with over-lap. This puts me in a good situation of being able to bridge cultural gabs and indeed perceiving reality from multiple angles.

The changes of the Western World are equally worrisome as those of the East. In the West, right now, right wing nationalism is increasing in many places, hand in hand with xenophobia and Islamophobia. I personally find that as concerning as religious fundamentalism.

What are your thoughts on being queer and Muslim. How do you reconcile the two?

Again, I was very lucky by having encountered some Sufi teachers, whose ideas about Islam and homosexuality were rather progressive and accepting, who explained things to me in a different light than the average fossilized Mullah. Combined with my happy years living in the Arab World, and having enjoyed wonderful relationships, I managed to achieve a harmonic integrity of all my aspects where spirituality and sensuality form a holistic totality, not being fragmented or at war. Plus, I also love and accept myself, which is really a vital point and a must. So I think the main credit for achieving this must go to the Sufi Tradition, as it really is the main helper and positive impact.

That is a wonderful place to be. You still travel a lot, and have recently been to Muslim majority countries like Morocco and Turkey. I'm sure you encounter queer Muslims who are not where you're at in your reconciliation of your identities.

Yes, that's true. Sadly enough I have encountered quite a number of queer Muslims who are rather troubled. There is the type who hates himself and would like to be white or straight or both. Or there is the type who cut off all religious and spiritual aspects, going into hardcore denial of any form of spirituality. I find that quite tragic.

Having issues with our identities is not really limited to being a queer Muslim in the Muslim World. In your memoir, "Khalil & Majnun," Khalil is suffering from an acute form of identity crises. He is no longer Muslim exactly, but a large part of his identity is Muslim. The reader can't help but feel emphatic to his suffering, but what is it like being around someone like that in a "free" society in the heart of Europe?

Yeah, Khalil's troubles were rather surreal and somewhat overwhelming for me, especially in the context of being in the supposed free world. But then again our respective background stories and upbringings were very different, like night and day. Also, our reactions to external impacts varied tremendously: he internalized white British ideals and tried to live up to them, while I reject anything oppressive coming from outside of myself. I'm a rebel par excellence and don't want to conform.

Queer Jihad

Speaking of identities, your documentary film "Identities" is dealing with this issue. Not about being queer and Muslim, but about identities in general. If I didn't know you I would probably assume it's a therapeutic process of some sort. What inspired you to make a film about identity?

Actually it wasn't therapeutic for me personally, as at that time I already worked out my own identity mosaic. But I was fascinated with the theme per se and wanted to find out what others thought and felt in this regard. In the very beginning of that process I met Khalil and the idea was to have him involved in the film and at the same time turn possibly into some therapy for him. I guess in those days I also had a strong helper syndrome. Anyway, he quickly got cold feet and ran away and the rest is history.

In retrospect, how do you feel about what happened with him?

Actually, right now, from my current perspective, I'm very happy about how the cookie crumbled, both for my film and emotionally for me as a person too. At this point I'm in a different space and I clearly know what I want and what I don't want, and I'd rather be a happy single than dreaming of getting involved in an unhappy relationship with a self-hater. But, by all fairness, I have to say thank you to Khalil for having inspired me on many levels in a quite "majnun" or crazy way. Perhaps that was his roll at the time and nothing else? Allah knows!

You're an artist engaged in a broad spectrum of activities in the arts. How did you end up in that world?

I strongly believe that people are born as artists. I'm certainly of that type, it showed at an early age when I already began to draw and paint and play music. As a matter of fact, I always knew that what I truly wanted to do with my life in terms of work was being an artist. Not a specialized one-way-street artist, but a multi-media artist. I'm inspired by the Renaissance spirit where artists like Leonardo da Vinci were also more than one thing. Most people might not be aware that he painted, sculpted, and even invented!

Does that conflict with the "mainstream" art world of today?

Unfortunately, our age promotes too many over-specialized people. I was already a misfit at art school and I'll continue being a misfit until I drop dead. My approach is cultural fusion and using any media. I see myself as much as a painter/photographer/visual artist as a musical composer, designer, writer or filmmaker. Many have said to me, "You can't do that!" But I counter with, "Yes, I can and I will!" I wouldn't be able to say good-bye to any aspects. I just go through phases where the focus is slightly different. So in short, I'm not a friend of categories and "isms" and probably being the marketing nightmare of some people on the business front.

In what ways do you think you would be nightmare for marketing people?

For example, I refuse to be labeled a European artist. Nor would it be correct to try and limit me with an Arab label. My motto is "neither of the East nor of the West." I'm a wild cultural cocktail, a fusion, and that is the very essence and the gist inspiring my art, no matter if I make a film or write a book or paint a picture or compose a piece of fusion world music or design some funky fusion fashion.

My aim is to be as universal and global as possible, and that is why I'm strongly opposed to any forms of nationalism. I don't even believe in citizenships and passports, a passport is a piece of paper, I'm a holder of one, no more, you shall never hear me say I'm this, that or the other nationality. But, I gladly and proudly say I'm a nomad and I'm an artist with my emotional and cultural background roots in the Arab and Latino world. So, yeah, it's a bit nightmare for the current day marketing people.

Most people who are not artists think art is fun and not a real work. But art can be a difficult profession, both physically and psychologically. I know it may not be easy to answer this, but which art are you most comfortable working with?

Queer Jihad

Art might have aspects of being fun, but indeed it is also hard work. I can easily answer your question: I have no choice. For me, art is always entering into a trance-like state of inspiration and in that sense it really doesn't matter if I happen to be inspired to create a piece of music, to paint, or work on a film or write. Even if all these arts are technically different, the creative process is really the same, no matter what. And when I get an urge to create, I do have to do it without delay; something else is taking over and I feel utterly comfortable to surrender to this process of artistic giving birth.

Your book, "Khalil & Majnun," could you tell the reader a little information about it.

Most people have heard about Leila and Majnun, a classical Sufi literature piece, which originally started off as an Bedouin-Arab poem, followed by Nizami's version in Farsi, etc. My book is a contemporary Sufi story in that vein, written in English, a queer variation in the form of a memoir.

What should we expect from you next?

My second book is scheduled to be released in the Spring of 2012, entitled "Hussein & The Nomad," and a bunch of my films are coming out too.

In every interview, I ask this last question: if you had the power to change something about yourself, what would it be and why?

Physically I wouldn't change anything about myself, but I would make myself a slightly more patient person, and if I had the power this time around I won't leave Brazil and continue to stay with Ulysses in Bahia, *"para fazer uma boa..."*

UPDATE: Since this interview was conducted Rahal Ek's book "Hussein & The Nomad" was published. His next book, "On the Path of the Friend" is expected to be released in the spring of 2015. In the meantime, his documentary film on various people about their identities, entitled "Identities," was released in 2013, as well as short films that were part of international collections. His next film, "Go West," about a Chinese artist who migrates to Berlin, is being released in 2014. He's currently plotting where to move next.

FARIS MALIK

Faris Malik's website, "'Born Eunuchs' Home Page and Library," features a section on Islam, which is a popular section for LGBT Muslims as it introduces holy texts with a new focus. For many years now, he has also been the webmaster of "Queer Jihad" and its related forum on the Yahoo groups, which originally was created by Sulayman X. Despite having a linguistic background (he has degrees in German from Berkeley and Princeton), Faris has had interest in sexual minorities, eunuchs, and their respective histories since the early 1990s.

Tell me the story behind your Muslim name.

Faris Malik is basically a translation of my legal given name, Mark Andrew, which means "horse" and "man", and my father's name, Donald, which means "world ruler." When I converted to Islam, my boyfriend at the time, also a convert, felt a person ought to have a Muslim name in Arabic. So with his advice on the proper form, I came up with one. Plus, I liked the idea of myself as a horseman or knight trying to find a holy grail and to right historical wrongs through my research into sexuality, history and religion.

Do you remember anything about Islam from growing up?

My first stepfather, back in the early seventies when I was in elementary school, was a Muslim sympathizer at least, if not actually a convert. Because of his identification with Islam, he forbade us to eat pork. He occasionally went to a Nation of Islam temple in San Francisco—he was Black, so that was not so weird—and often sent me to buy day-old bread at the Shabazz bakery. Even after my mom left him, we kept avoiding pork because of what he had told us about how unhealthy it was. Over the years, Islam remained present in the back of my mind as a potential alternative way of thinking about God, although I never knew much about it or paid it much attention until my late twenties and early thirties.

Queer Jihad

When did you decide to become a Muslim, and why?

While still going to various Christian churches, I had started giving a lot of thought to the seeming contradiction between God's love for human beings, His creation of gay people, and the fierce condemnation of homosexuality by the Christian religion and, apparently, by the Bible. In that context, I began researching sexuality in the ancient world and found a way to resolve that contradiction that I believe is historically accurate. Eventually I found ancient textual evidence that proves to my mind that, when Jesus spoke of "born eunuchs," he was referring to the type of man I think of as born gay.

Anyway, right after I found that evidence, I met and started dating my Muslim boyfriend, who was having trouble reconciling his being gay with his religion. I decided to see what the Qur'an said about homosexuality, and found that the Qur'an upheld the type of resolution of the problem that I had uncovered in my research, and that in fact the Qur'an very subtly avoided condemning homosexuality as practiced between innately gay men. That convinced me the Qur'an was, in part, a divine correction of an injustice perpetrated by the Catholic Church when it became the dominant force in the Roman Empire.

I still didn't become a Muslim until I read the whole Qur'an and discovered that God was very upset about the Christian doctrine of the trinity and the assertion that God begot Himself in the form of Jesus. That made it impossible for me to continue attending a Christian church. But I am not a very devout practicing Muslim in the conventional sense. The word Muslim means one who is obedient to God, and I try to live my life that way. But to my mind that does not mean following so-called *shari'ah* or imitating the Prophet. One of my favorite *ayats* is the one saying that God's words are more than could be written down with two oceans of ink (Surah 18:109). The Qur'an and all hadith collections could be printed with a single print cartridge . That means we have to open our minds to all sources of truth, not just religious scriptures.

Your website is a resourceful place for those interested in gender, sexuality and faith. What has been the response to the Muslim sections of it?

The response has been mostly positive, although not many Muslims, or people in general for that matter, are aware of my website at all. I occasionally google "Faris Malik" to see what people are saying about my site, and I have to say that when people do refer to my site, their comments are generally positive, whether coming from Muslims or non-Muslims. My pages, including the page specifically about queer identity in the Qur'an and hadith, have been linked dozens of times on the web. As for criticism, the only consistent critique I have seen from Muslims, or anyone else for that matter, is to cast doubt on my credibility as a researcher. But of course, my credentials as a researcher are irrelevant to the validity of the research. So far, no one has gone to the trouble of disputing the evidence I present.

On top of your own website, you're also running the "Queer jihad" website, which Sulayman used to get a lot of threats in e-mail for. Are those kinds of comments still coming?

Sulayman turned over the management of "Queer Jihad" to me back in 2002, and one of his conditions was that he asked me to preserve the often harshly negative comments that he had collected, which I reluctantly agreed to do. But I really have had hardly any comments about the site. People still write letters of thanks and encouragement to Sulayman, like once a year maybe, but I have only had a handful of condemning emails in all these years, which are rarely more than a line or two saying I am going to hell or something like that. I never get any kind of reasoned argument against what Sulayman or I have posted, but I do get appreciative letters every so often.

You are working on a book, now for many years... tell me about that.

Um... are you asking me to tell you about the book, or about why I have been slacking about getting it done? Seriously, though, the book will essentially be a history of the shift in understanding of the homosexual type over the centuries between the ancient pagan world, when same-sex desire was expressed and acted upon widely among the general population, and the modern world, when the general population denies any same-sex desires.

In ancient times, when homosexual activity between men and teenage boys was widespread, actual homosexual men, as we understand them today, were set apart from the norm because of their lack of potency with women rather than because of the sexual desires that they felt for other men. That lack of potency with women entailed a difference in gender between innately and exclusively homosexual men and the general population of men, who could and did go both ways, such that exclusively homosexual men were considered not to be "male" at all, but rather to be natural eunuchs.

The funny thing is, as much as we are led to believe that the Bible and the Qur'an condemn homosexual activity per se, they never do. The scriptures, not to mention ancient pagan laws around the world, never condemn homosexual activity in general. But they do condemn the sexual penetration of "males." So it is true, as many gay liberation theologians claim, that ancient laws, including the scriptures, do not condemn sex between exclusively gay men, or when exclusively gay men are penetrated. But, on the other hand, they do condemn sex in which men are penetrated who might at other times have sex with women. That is not a welcome argument, either for people who believe in full sexual liberation or for people who believe in strict heterosexuality.

It is taking so long to write the book because, as simple as that argument is, there are a lot of cherished misconceptions out there about human sexuality—many of which contradict each other—and it will take a huge amount of evidence, convincingly presented, to overcome those misconceptions. For instance, most average gay people do not believe that "straight" people feel homosexual attractions, even though they keep telling us that they do.

To see a lighthearted example of how they tell us, just check out the sexual tension among Chandler, Joey, and Ross on the TV show "Friends." Of course, they are fictional characters, but they are written by real straight people. Gay people would think that the comedy in their frequent stumbles into male-male affection comes from their inordinate fear of being perceived as gay. Straights would recognize that the comedy really comes from their fears of their straightness being betrayed by their real desires for closeness with their male friends, which might at any moment take them too far. Many gay people believe the essentialist argument that if you feel homosexual desires, you must be gay. And if you are gay, you ought to come out about it. Conversely, many straight people, even the ones who are "straight but not narrow," feel that homosexual or heterosexual identity is a matter of behavior rather than essence. What makes them "straight" is just their behavior, not the configuration of their unexpressed desires.

To give an example of the different perception, both gays and straight might conclude that Sen. Larry Craig is a closet homosexual because he was caught trolling bathrooms for sex with men. But gays will think he is homosexual because by nature he was attracted to men sexually, and supposedly only gay men are attracted to other men. Straights, on the other hand, will think he is a homosexual only because he took action to put his attraction to men into practice. If he had kept his attraction in check and refused to act on it, they would not think him any different by nature than any other straight man.

Straights and gays have fundamentally different senses of their sexual options. Straights can choose between heterosexuality, homosexuality, or bisexuality, and they choose heterosexuality. Most gays have only a choice between homosexuality or no sexuality at all. Yet each group falsely projects its own experience onto the other, mutatis mutandi. Not to say that there aren't bisexuals who choose a strictly gay lifestyle and identify as gay. But those gays would probably call their homosexuality a preference rather than an orientation.

Like I said, my basic argument is simple to state, but hard to bring across, because there are so many preconceptions to overcome out there. Not to mention the fact that most gay men don't want to think of themselves as eunuchs, even though eunuchs had a rich and powerful history in centuries past.

Very interesting stuff. What is next for you?

My next work assignment. I work as a freelance translator. I want to make the time to write, but having to make a living keeps getting in the way. Writing is a hard habit to get into.

In every interview, I ask this last question: if you had the power to change something about yourself, what would it be and why?

I wish I had more self-discipline. It's hard to force myself to do anything unless I am up against a short-term deadline.

SHARIFA ISMAIL

If you want to meet a unique person, meet Sharifa Ismail. I was introduced to her by a friend of mine and she and I became friends very quickly, mostly because we share a deep common concern for the queer Muslim community. She spent most of her life supporting causes that help the community, yet she is so private that even some people she financially supports have never met her. Over the years, she was the largest financial supporter of the Arabic edition of *Huriyah*, and which she financed exclusively for some years. She had been the main financial support of *Hamd*, a support group for queer women in Egypt, since the 1970s even though she is not even Egyptian (she is Iraqi). She is a woman who puts her money where her mouth is, and it was a pleasure to interview her.

How is life in Iraq for a lesbian?

It is impossible. *Life*, I mean. There is a difference between being alive and just getting by. In the past and the present, a lesbian gets by in Iraq.

You were married to a man at the age of fourteen. How was that?

I went through it. It was something that God thought I should go through.

Do you really think God wanted a 14-year-old lesbian to be married off to a man twice her age?

In Islam, God wills everything, good and bad. I have to believe that God saw good in that experience for me. Marriage showed me that I was truly a lesbian. Before the marriage, I wasn't sure. After the first night of the marriage, I was pretty sure! It was the most uncomfortable night in my entire life. I don't want to get graphic, so I will keep it clean. He rapped me, violently. The next morning I

185

told the situation to my mother and she said that it happens that way to most Iraqi women. When asked why she didn't warn me, she said that it was something I had to discover for myself.

Do most Iraqi women experience this today? I mean, is it still the same way?

No. Now more and more women are marrying for love, or at least men they have chosen. When I was a young woman, Iraqi women didn't choose but were chosen for. My niece, for example, has married a man she loves. Lesbian Arabs are still marrying men they don't love, obviously.

So, how did your marriage go?

Well, it didn't last. After not having children for five years, he finally divorced me. I remember singing when I was told I was divorced. I must have been the happiest divorced woman in the world.

Tell me how the two of you (you and your partner Aisha) met.

After the divorce, I left the village and opened a coffee shop in Baghdad. Ten years later, she walked in one day. We are still together. Allah has been gracious to me. I fell in love with her that first day. The next day, I sold my coffee shop. A week later, we went to her country because it was better than Iraq. People are more independent in Yemen. You mind your own business. Of course, that is why Yemen has a reputation of being a cold country among the Arabs. As far as I am concerned, I think Yemen is wonderful. It is not about being cold, it is about living in reality. Later, when my mother died we moved back to Iraq.

I spoke to Aisha and she can't explain why you two were so attracted to one another. Can you try to give a reason or some way to understand how you two fell in love so quickly?

I really cannot. Love cannot be explained. It is supernatural. Aisha was just everything I wanted. This was very clear to me from the first moment we met. When we met, we looked at each other in a way only Aisha and I know. She initiated a hug and I didn't let her go. She said something that always was with me: "I'm here." Imagine this was a woman I have never seen prior to that meeting.

Aisha was not a Muslim when you met her, right?

No, she was an Eastern Orthodox Christian. We were together for a year before she converted. I never even asked her to consider it. The way I lived my life, as a Muslim, attracted her. She said that she found peace in the way I related to God and His creations.

Aisha said that your faith was always strong in God, where did that come from? I mean, was your family religious?

No. My father was a shoemaker. Mother was homemaker. Siblings were troublemakers and I was the fantasymaker. While my sibling fought over fake toys, I reached beyond the physical world and found peace and solutions. It was my childhood that I encountered God in such a deep and personal way.

Your sons. How did they come into your life?

They were orphans. Their parents were killed during a village war near the border with Iran. We adopted them through friends. One of my friends ran the orphanage house where the boys were kept. She said that I and my partner were not married, but because we could afford to give these children homes that she could overlook that fact. There weren't any lies involved. I didn't want them to be given to us through lies. So, we told the truth as much as we could. We didn't tell them we were lesbians, but we told them that we lived together and planned to live together.

How old were they?

They were babies when we got them. Hassan was two years old, and Hussein was just nine months. Of course, they are now all grown and don't even think they were ever in such state.

One of them is married, correct?

Yes, Hassan is married with two children. Hussein, the younger one, is still studying.

They are not gay.

Queer Jihad

No, I don't think so.

My mentor and good friend was telling me one day that gay friends of his say, "what did we do wrong?" of their straight kids, joking, of course.

Aisha says they are repressing their homosexuality. She tells the older one that he made a big mistake by marrying a woman. Yes, we like to have fun with them too. We are a good family and always were except that time when we were disrupted.

The Iraqi government separated you. Tell me about that.

Well, they accused us of living immoral lives and officially kicked Aisha out of the country. Her name was put on some list so she couldn't come to the country. I was jailed for three months. I was to be under house arrest for the next ten years. After that, I was told if I left the country I would never be allowed to return to it. We were separated for fifteen years. It was very hard. I slept crying many nights. We wrote back and forth letter but the letters came once a month, because by the time I receive hers and responded it would be a month already.

That is so awful. Aisha moved to Canada where she received asylum. Was it easier to communicate once she was in the West?

Oh, no, it was even harder then because the gulf war was going on when Aisha got into Canada. All communications with the outside world was crumbled.

Aisha tells me that the first time you two met after twenty and some years, you were both speechless, literally!

Yes, we didn't talk for a whole day. We just cried and hugged a lot. Every time I saw her eyes I cried.

You say the war [The Gulf War, 1991] gave you your life back, how so?

It allowed me to go back and forth in the country. The system was not as strict anymore. The government was more interested in hunting for people they identified as the enemy within than a lesbian old lady. Then, I went to the United Arab Emirates. It became easier to get to another Arab country. Aisha was able to bring us to Canada. I was shaking in the airplane.

Let's go back to the Arab World. You are involved with *Hamd*. **As I understand it, the organization was started in Egypt and you are Iraqi, so what am I missing?**

Well, I had a good friend from Egypt, she is dead now, God bless her soul. She was a lesbian. She was the one who introduced me to Farduz, the founder. Farduz and I became good friends and I joined the group. From that point on, I had to come to Cairo every six months for the meetings. In the beginning, it was very hard, financially, but was deeply healing for me. Those women healed wounds that were not even known to me. Deep wounds, the kind you don't reach for years.

Tell the reader what exactly *Hamd* **is and what it does.**

It's a support group for women who love other women. It was started in the 1960s by Farduz. She was what I call a fierce fem. She was everything we wanted to be: beautiful, gentle, feminine, and fierce! I met them many years later through an Egyptian friend and I was one of the few non-Egyptians who came regularly.

The women do many things, but most of their services are about supporting each other. They meet, they have parties, they console each other, and all that is needed. Some women come there so they can actually smoke in the company of these women, or simply even drink wine—things they are not allowed to do at home. Some women come because they like how they feel in the company of Muslim women who are not afraid to identify as lesbian.

You're currently considered the oldest member in the group in terms of the years you're with them, but does that mean you're still attending meetings, are you traveling to Egypt even in this period?

I generally attend through phone conferencing nowadays. It has been some years since I was physically with the women. But I will definitely be a member of that group until I leave this earth.

Queer Jihad

These women are my family, they are my sisters and my daughters and my friends.

What scares you the most?

Life without Aisha. I'm terrified of that. I always hope I'm the one to go first.

In every interview that I do, I ask this last question: If you had the power to change something about yourself, what would it be, and why?

I would be a better cook. I mess up the simplest recipes.

UPDATE: This interview was originally conducted in 2002, and Sharifa has since moved back to Iraq with Aisha.

About the Author

Afdhere Jama was born in Somalia and immigrated to the United States when he was a teenager. He is the author of "Illegal Citizens: Queer Lives in the Muslim World," and was the editor of *Huriyah*, which was the first magazine for and by queer Muslims. He lives in California.

Glossary of Terms

Al-Fatiha - The first chapter of the Qur'an. First LGBT Muslim organization in the United States was named Al-Fatiha.

Alhamdulillah - Phrase Muslims use, meaning Praise is for God.

Dhikr - Sufi exercises, might include meditation or reciting internally or externally verses, or the names of God, or focusing on a particular task. In most cultures it also might include musical expression of the same.

Dunya - Muslim expression about the world. In Arabic, *dunya* means world.

Fajr - The first Muslim ritual prayer of the day, at dawn.

Hadith - The collected material in which many sourced individuals claim to have heard what Prophet Muhammad said about many subjects, often divided into *saheeh* or authentic and *da'eef* or weak.

Hajj - Muslim pilgrimage to Mecca.

Haram - Something forbidden in Islam.

Hijab - A way for people to cover. Depending on various codes in various branches of the faith, often regulated by cultural understanding of modesty.

Imam - A Muslim religious leader, especially often one leads a particular mosque.

Jihad - A struggle, both internal and external, violent and peaceful. For example, Ghandi's nonviolent *Satyagraha* is called jihad in Arabic.

Juma - Friday ritual prayer, taking place at midday.

Khutba - Lecture given just before Friday's ritual prayer at midday.

Muharram - Muslim New Year.

Nafs - Sufi understanding of different levels of the self. In Arabic, *nafs* means soul.

Nikah - Muslim marriage.

Rahim - Short for *Al-Rahim*, The Most Merciful, one of the 99 attributes of God.

Salaam - A word in Arabic that means peace, which Muslims use as a greeting. It's also the first openly support group for LGBT Muslims, found by El-Farouk Khaki in 1991 in Canada.

Salafi - A follower of a strict orthodox form of Islam.

Salat - Muslim ritual prayers.

Sharia - Moral code and religious law of Muslims. It deals with both personal and communal issues, and is diverse as it's regulated by the different branches of the faith.

Shahadah - Muslim declaration of faith.

Sheikh - A title given to someone who officially studied the faith.

Suggested Readings

Islamic Homosexualities: Culture, History, and Literature by Will Roscoe and Stephen O. Murray (1997, New York University Press)

Gay Travels in the Muslim World by Michael Luongo (2007, Routledge)

Illegal Citizens: Queer Lives in the Muslim World by Afdhere Jama (2008, Oracle Releasing)

Islam and Homosexuality by Samar Habib (2009, Praeger)

Before Homosexuality in the Arab-Islamic World, 1500-1800 by Khaled El-Rouayheb (2009, University of Chicago Press)

Homosexuality in Islam: Critical Reflection on Gay, Lesbian, and Transgender Muslims by Scott Siraj al-Haqq Kugle (2010, Oneworld Publicatins)

www.ingramcontent.com/pod-product-compliance
Lightning Source LLC
LaVergne TN
LVHW041542070426
835507LV00011B/882